REDISCOVERY

Western Canada Wilderness Committee

Author: Thom Henley
Editor: Athena George
Illustrations and Design: Debbie Duncan
Photographs: Thom Henley
Cover photo: Walter and Diane Maile
Title page: Haida bracelet design, Clarence Mills
All other contributors of text, illustrations, and photographs are gratefully credited within the book. Typeset by Vanguard Publishing. Printed in Canada by Hemlock Printers.

Published by Western Canada Wilderness Committee, 20 Water Street, Vancouver, British Columbia, Canada V6B 1A4. A portion of the profit from the sale of each copy of this book goes to Rediscovery International Foundation's support of all Rediscovery-affiliated camps.

Canadian Cataloguing in Publication Data
Henley, Thom, 1948-
   Rediscovery

   Includes index.
   ISBN 0-9692230-3-X

   1. Outdoor education. 2. Environmental education.
3. Indians of North America — Philosophy. I. Western Canada Wilderness Committee. II. Title.
LB1047.H45 1989   371.3'8   C89-091212-2

REDISCOVERY

ANCIENT PATHWAYS — NEW DIRECTIONS

A Guidebook to Outdoor Education

THOM HENLEY

*This book is lovingly dedicated
to the elders, whose tradition of sharing
has given the world a most remarkable gift.*

CONTENTS

FOREWORD
By Bill Reid

It was late fall or early winter, although you would never know it. The sky was overcast. It was short-sleeve weather, warm, calm, and very peaceful. A small pack of kids eight or nine years old were doing what kids have been doing for the last five thousand years in front of this village, coursing their way eagerly along the beach, rattling the gravel and leaving heel prints in the sand, splashing most gratifyingly through streamlets and tidal pools.

Jimmy Hart and I were restoring the totem that decorates the front of the band office. The pack stopped near us and drifted about whispering in their strange secret language, and one of them picked up a tool and began carving a piece of driftwood. We were not very interested in our job, so instead of sending them down the beach, we distributed our tools among them and put them to work carving small boats. They stayed with us about an hour and during that time their skills improved at least fivefold; and because they were so involved in their manual tasks they spoke very freely and unself-consciously of their lives, ambitions, relationships with their families, and so on. Then they got bored and went off down the beach as children had been doing for thousands of years.

With one difference; on this long beach, on that warm winter day, Jimmy, the kids, and I were the only human beings to be seen. Some evidence of life could be deduced from the electronic flickers seen through the windows of many of the houses, but that was all.

For all the preceding centuries that man has lived on this stretch of coastline, even a hundred years ago, the beach would have been the scene of constant and varied activity. In front of every house, someone would have been building a canoe, or carving a totem pole, or preserving food — occupied with the countless activities necessary to sustaining the rich and colourful lives of the Haida.

The kids would have been a part of the whole scene, used as casual help as their skills permitted, learning something of the knowledge essential to their future lives from the vast talents that their community

Rediscovery allows for trips up and down the beach, where the learning of traditions can still take place.

had to offer. A thousand trips up and down the beach would probably be sufficient to make each of them a universal man or woman, admittedly of a small universe, but they would have a working knowledge of all the techniques developed through the centuries by which the Haidas coped with their environment, as well as complete knowledge of the language and legends of their kind.

Perhaps the descriptions rooted in myth of the origins of this universe seem fanciful and inexact compared to the scientific logic we follow. Both give order and structure to the world and its happening, and if mankind didn't emerge from the Clamshell at the urging of the Raven exactly as described, there's no reason to believe that the land bridge so conveniently appeared and disappeared in that other story. But who knows, this may be another myth.

The wonderful thing about Rediscovery is that it has enabled all these different truths to exist side by side. It provides for a few more trips up and down the beach where traditional teaching can still take place, and helps young people whose private universes seem empty and chaotic to discover there is some order in their lives and their world. And even if there isn't, some may be inspired to turn the raw material of chaos into structured hope for the future.

Bill Reid, February 1989
Bill Reid, Haida elder and internationally acclaimed artist, has been supportive of Rediscovery for many years.

FOREWORD
By David Suzuki

Like most of the people living in North America today, I am a non-native. My ancestors came to Canada from Japan at the turn of the century. Like most recent immigrants, my grandparents saw in the land the possibility for possession and profit. They came out of dire poverty intending to make a fortune and return to Japan as wealthy people. They had no intention of settling in this "barbaric" country, but, like many others with similar plans, they stayed.

North America, to the native people living here, is more than simply a place, a piece of turf. Land embodies culture, history, and the remains of distant ancestors. Land is the source of all life and the basis of identity. Land is sacred. An overriding sense in aboriginal perceptions is that of gratitude for nature's bounty and beauty. Gratitude — and respect.

Land in modern North America is currently regarded as a commodity, to be purchased, exploited for its resources, and sold for profit. Land, for most people, does not embody cultural history. Land is profane. Indeed, to refrain from exploiting an opportunity to log, mine, farm, or otherwise develop is an obscenity, a waste.

Our modern land ethic is causing a cataclysmic upheaval on this planet. Species of plants and animals are becoming extinct thousands of times faster than has ever occurred before; their habitats destroyed by human beings. Global deforestation is causing vast changes in the patterns of water availability, weather, climate, and soils. Human-caused desertification is accelerating. Massive global pollution is putting not only other life forms but even our own children's health at risk.

Twenty percent of the world's population — the industrialized countries — are now utilizing over eighty percent of the planet's exploited resources, and they continue to demand even more, in growing consumption and profits.

From an ecological perspective, *Homo sapiens* is a species temporarily out of biological control. We are now the most numerous and ubiquitous large mammal in the world. But armed with the muscle power of science and technology, our impact on the planet is beyond

11

Rediscovery puts people in touch with the beauty and complexity of nature.

anything ever experienced in the history of life on earth. We have initiated an "extinction spasm" that Harvard ecologist E.O. Wilson estimates now claims over seventeen thousand species a year.

Stanford ecologist Paul Ehrlich calculates that human beings now marshal for their own use forty percent of the planet's *net primary productivity* (NPP — all the energy fixed through photosynthesis each year). The NPP is the basic source of life on earth, and the more NPP we use the more we crowd out other species.

If our species' fecundity is not curbed, we will double our population within fifty years. Ten billion humans would use eighty percent of the global NPP — an unfathomable ecological catastrophe. To use a medical metaphor, our species' rapid spread, increase in size, rapacious consumption of the planet's resources, and destruction of many of the life forms around us has all the characteristics of a malignant cancer within the biosphere.

Why are we destroying the very support systems for all life on Earth? Apart from our powerful urge for profit, it is our lack of sacred respect for the land and the other life forms sharing our habitat that exacerbates the problem. Today, over eighty percent of North Americans live in

Young people experience a sense of the earth as home, and feel connected to all other living things.

cities, man-made environments that have been created by us according to our ideas of beauty and utility. In the countryside, the fields, orchards, pastures, and even forests have been manicured and managed to meet human needs. This creates an illusion that we have the knowledge and the power to control nature. Indeed, in urban settings, "weeds," "pests," and "vermin" — animals and plants that defy human control — are seen as dangerous, dirty, or disgusting.

Essentially, nature has become alien, an enemy, and we live with a terrible delusion that somehow we are different, no longer subject to the same rules that govern all other life forms. We have lost all sense of belonging in nature and have become intoxicated with the short-term benefits of science and technology that have bludgeoned nature into apparent submission.

But in spite of all our great achievements in science and technology, we remain incredibly ignorant about the natural world. We have only identified 1.4 million of perhaps 30 million species in the world, and, of those we do know, we have little knowledge about their basic biology.

In order to stop our blind rush down the present pathway, we have to undergo a profound change in attitude and perception. We have to first identify ourselves, again, as animals. Like all other animals, we require clean air, water, and earth. We are members of an ecosystem in which stability and continuity are possible only when we stay in balance with other living creatures.

Clearly, we also need a renewed sense of earth as home; belonging to the land, connected to all other living things. This is why I believe that the Rediscovery program is so important. Youngsters today have few, if any, opportunities to experience the enormity and beauty of wilderness — Rediscovery offers them that. Few of us know our own capacity for the ingenuity and inventiveness required in the fundamental process of living — Rediscovery reveals that. Overwhelmed by a multiplicity of consumer products, we seldom have a chance to see how few are really important or necessary — Rediscovery shows that.

Most important, Rediscovery provides access to ancient wisdom in native cultures. In spite of centuries of oppression and exploitation by European culture, many native people have clung to the attitudes of their ancestors. Their sense of the sanctity of the land — as their home and as the source of history, culture, and life itself — expresses a belief and value system which is radically different, and which we must all rediscover to help deflect us from our headlong rush to destruction.

As a parent, environmentalist, and scientist, I cannot conceive of a more important program than Rediscovery. Everyone in North America, old and young, should have the chance to take part. Read this book and find out what it's all about.

David Suzuki, February 1989
David Suzuki, award-winning geneticist, and host of the national television program, The Nature of Things, *has been adopted by Stein Rediscovery as an honourary elder.*

INTRODUCTION
Different Pathways

Each of us have our own discoveries and re-discoveries in life — profound personal experiences which renew our inner spirit, re-awaken in us a desire to know and understand other cultures, and rekindle a sense of wonder in the natural world. I know I have had many. I grew up in Lansing, Michigan, a stone's throw from the belching smokestacks of the Oldsmobile factory. It was not the richest natural environment I might have been born into nor was it the poorest. There was one small vacant lot in my old neighbourhood, overgrown with trees and brush, fallen leaves and limbs, that was, for me, in my childhood imagination, a wilderness. The lot was bordered on two sides by houses, and on the other two by a garbage-strewn alley and the city's busiest street. But when I was low to the ground, buried in weeds and close to the earthy aroma of moulding oak leaves, fungus, and soil, I imagined that I was in the wildest place on earth. In my mind's eye, there were still deer and bear and wolverine roaming these wilds, even though wolverine had been extinct in Michigan (the Wolverine State) long before I was born. I tried to imagine Indians living in such a place and dreamed of finding an arrowhead or some other sign of early habitation. But the native nations of lower Michigan had almost been swept from memory. To me, Indians appeared as distant as the ancient Egyptians, even though an encampment of wigwams might well have occupied the site of my neighbourhood not long ago.

I found another outlet for my wilderness yearnings and fascination with native cultures in the Scouting program, progressing from Cub to Eagle Scout and collecting all the necessary merit badges in between. But it wasn't the system of advancement or the patriotism or the military-styled marches, salutes, and uniforms that commanded my loyalty to Scouts, it was the opportunity to further connect with the "wilds," even if that meant only woodlots surrounded by cornfields in the flat Midwest countryside, and to experience "Indian lore" — even if it was taught by white men dressed in Plains Indian regalia.

It wasn't until I left Michigan at the age of twenty and first set eyes on

Rediscovery's origins are the story of many people being led along many different pathways. Hikers arrive at Taalung Slung.

British Columbia, Alaska, and the Yukon that I finally understood the true meaning of wilderness, and came to know deep in my heart that I was home. I met Indians here, nations of people maintaining distinct languages, customs, and identity in spite of all efforts to assimilate them. For several years I totally immersed myself in the wilderness: kayaking arctic rivers, mushing dog-teams on winter expeditions in Alaska, building log cabins in remote reaches, and learning from bush pilots, trappers, prospectors, and native elders. I had always intended to go back and complete university, but I came to realize that education was where you found it, that nature itself was the greatest teacher and the earth the real university.

It wasn't until I first came to know Haida Gwaii (the Queen Charlotte Islands) that my re-discovering began in earnest. I had paddled the length of the Queen Charlotte Archipelago in my wood and canvas kayak, and was in the process of trying to cross the sixty-kilometre stretch of Dixon Entrance into Alaskan waters when a sudden storm forced me back to the shores of Haida Gwaii.

Without knowing my exact whereabouts, I made an emergency landing at the first safe refuge I could find. It was the long-abandoned

Haida village site of Yaku, sixty kilometres from the nearest town, road, or telephone. I was more than a little surprised, therefore, the next morning while clam digging, to find myself suddenly surrounded by a group of eight Haida kids. "What are *you* doing here?" they asked in surprise. "Digging clams," I answered. "What are you doing here?" I asked in return. "Watching you," came the sensible answer.

The young students were working at a nearby archaeological dig called Project Kiusta, and in the true tradition of Haida hospitality, they invited me back to their camp to share in lunch. It wasn't long before they had persuaded me to join them in their project — at least until the seas calmed enough to continue my journey north to Alaska. A few days later I was further persuaded to cross the narrow neck of land that separates Kiusta from the west coast to see a beautiful beach known, in Haida, as Taalung Slung. It was one of those experiences that cannot be conveyed in words, but which profoundly affects one's life. I was drawn to the site where the Rediscovery camp is located today and immediately set about building what would become the first staff cabin. This was not a conscious effort on my part, as there was no thought of a youth camp in my mind. The following spring I spent three months completely alone at Taalung Slung, finishing the cabin, exploring the wild west coast, and taking a journey of inner self that proved the greatest single experience of my life. It would be another four years before the Rediscovery camp came into being, but the stage was set for my involvement, and my own rediscovery had begun.

The story of Rediscovery's origins is the story of many people being led along many different paths. Some of the pathways are ancient. The ancestral Haidas that cared for the land and so carefully stewarded the resources that the first Rediscovery camp enjoys today, were certainly more significant contributors than anyone now living. For there is still the beauty and power of the land itself, the ancient rainforest, the abundant wildlife, the Pacific waves exploding on sea stacks and headlands, and the weathered totem poles being reclaimed by the forest at three nearby former village sites.

Even as a camp, Rediscovery did not suddenly spring into being; there were important predecessors on Haida Gwaii. The Project Kiusta archaeological dig had clearly demonstrated the feasibility of using such a remote location, and previous Haida summer camps (organized by the Haida band councils) had proven the value of such experiences to local youth. It required a huge community effort to launch Rediscovery in 1978, but once the pilot project began it became clear to many that something unique was beginning to evolve. Rediscovery was a camp for everyone: a broad range of ages, boys and girls, native and non-native, the privileged and underprivileged, those in a state of crisis and those well adjusted. Rediscovery's goals were as simple as they were all-encompassing: to discover the world within oneself, the cultural worlds between people, and the wonders of the natural world around us.

Of course, Haida Gwaii Rediscovery, as we know it today, is very different from that first-year pilot program. There was a naivete in those formative days in thinking that all youngsters brought to such a dynamic, diverse, and stunningly beautiful setting would immediately immerse themselves in fun and challenging activities. This was the television generation, however, with twenty-minute attention spans. During the often rainy weather, some teens gathered in their tents amidst piles of mouldy socks, playing cards, craving junk food and complaining of boredom. As much as the staff wanted to avoid regimented programming, some structure and organized activities were clearly called for.

Some Rediscovery staff brought with them experience gained at other nature camps, environmental education activities, and outdoor theatre. Others brought bush skills from years of wilderness experience and knowledge gained from contact with other cultures. The Haida elders brought a continuity with the past and the wisdom and skills necessary to carry time-honoured traditions into the future. Moreover, the Haida people began to share their love, their songs, legends, dances, and other traditions with non-native children as if they were children of their own. It was this act of sharing, more than any other factor, which made Rediscovery what it is today. Slowly, painstakingly, the program evolved.

Rediscovery was never envisioned expanding beyond the shores of Haida Gwaii, but other communities and tribal groups began viewing the camp as a model. When, in 1985, Rediscovery International Foundation was established to assist other communities in their program developments, a whole new evolution began. Rediscovery Four Corners, in the San Luis Valley of southern Colorado, was the first Rediscovery developed outside Haida Gwaii. The following year, two other programs were initiated, in the Stikine River region of northern British Columbia and the Stein Valley of south central B.C. In 1987, three more Rediscovery programs resulted from local community effort: Wind River, Wyoming, Bella Bella and Bella Coola, British Columbia. In the summer of 1988, two more Rediscovery camps opened, in Desolation Sound, British Columbia, and the Lake Athabascan region of northern Alberta. Several other programs are now in the developing stage: Rediscovery

Hawaii on the island of Kauai, Cheanuh Rediscovery on the southern tip of Vancouver Island, and Port Hardy Rediscovery on the north coast of Vancouver Island, British Columbia.

With these new developments came some new and interesting challenges. It is relatively easy to have a Haida Gwaii Rediscovery focusing on Haida culture, but what happens in an area like Rediscovery Four Corners where Lakota, Ute, Pueblo, and Navajo cultures all share in the same camp? The cross-cultural sensitivity required of native and non-native staff and participants becomes just as critical between different native nations — some of which must overcome traditional animosities or major cultural differences. As Lorraine Fox Davis, one of the founders of Rediscovery Four Corners, has said, "What one tribe takes lightly another may consider very serious. Cross-cultural sensitivity is so delicate a dance."

Rediscovery is no longer a single program, but rather a broad network of affiliated programs, each community-founded and -based, independently administered and funded, and uniquely suited to its bioregion and indigenous culture. While all Rediscovery programs meet agreed-upon health and safety standards, and none discriminate on the basis of race, sex, creed, or nationality, there are more distinctions than similarities between them. The reason for this, of course, is that Haida culture is as different from Ute or Pueblo culture as the wet west coast of Haida Gwaii differs from the desert alpine of Colorado's San Luis Valley. No two cultures and no two bioregions are ever alike, and Rediscovery programs reflect that wonderful diversity.

Rediscovery camps serve the needs of native as well as non-native youth within an authentic cultural context. These are not the standard summer camps where totem poles are propped in front of tipis as part of Indian lore. Any Rediscovery participant could tell you that such misrepresentations are as ridiculous as displaying the Eiffel Tower in front of the Taj Mahal. Cultural authenticity is integral to the Rediscovery experience. The indigenous peoples who host and help develop these programs are members of truly distinct nations with languages, religions, customs, and traditions every bit as different from one another as are any two cultures of Europe.

By drawing from the strength of native traditions, the wisdom of elders, a philosophy of respect and love for the land and each other, and with a focus on the spirituality of all life, Rediscovery emerges today as a new direction for youth camps.

This book has not been as easy to write as I had first hoped. Perhaps it is because Rediscovery origins are so distant, its focus all-encompassing, its applications so broad that it defies simple description. It is also a product of the heart more than the mind, a continuation of native tradition more than a contemporary innovation. Five native consultants from four Indian nations have reviewed this book and made valuable contributions to its content. Through their help, this book hopes to share the joys of Rediscovery, not only with the large and growing family directly affiliated through the camps, but with the extended human family at large.

HOW TO USE THIS BOOK

How you use this book, as with any guidebook, depends on what you want from it. If you simply want to find out about Rediscovery, then you may browse through, looking at the photos and reading what catches your eye. If you are a teacher preparing to take your class to an outdoor camp for a week, you might be looking for outdoor activities, checking the Quick Activity Guide. If you plan to develop a youth camp in your community, then you'll probably read over the Rediscovery model, the checklist of how to develop a Rediscovery of your own, and the address of the nearest Rediscovery camp.

To help you decide how you want to use this book, here is a description of the three major parts. In Part I, we will explore some traditional native approaches to nature and their relevance to contemporary life. We will also detail the underlying principles of Rediscovery. The core of the book, Part II, consists of eighty activities used in the Rediscovery program. They are divided into three groups: personal, cultural, and environmental awareness. The activities are not expected to be used in any particular order and can be adapted to suit different settings, cultures, and ages. Part III profiles the Rediscovery camps now in operation and development, reviews the guidelines for a community wishing to develop a Rediscovery of its own, and discusses the ways everyone can assist in keeping the Rediscovery circle — the international network of camps — financially secure and strong.

PART I

NATIVE PATHWAYS TO NATURE

The Lakota was a true Naturist
— a lover of Nature;
he loved the earth and all things of the earth,
the attachment growing with age.

The old Lakota was wise.
He knew that man's heart away from Nature becomes hard.
He knew that lack of respect for growing, living things
soon led to lack of respect for humans too.
So he kept his youth close to its softening influence.

— Chief Luther Standing Bear (Lakota)

Salmon design, Lionel Samuels

CHAPTER 1
BELONGING TO THE EARTH

There has, perhaps, never been a time in history when humankind has been more removed from the natural world. More and more of us live, work, and travel in rigidly controlled artificial environments. We eat food so far removed from its source that it is difficult to imagine it was once an animal or plant at all. Answers to nature's secrets are sought in sterile laboratories, windowless rooms with fluorescent lighting and rigidly controlled atmospheres. And sometimes parts of answers are found. But the wholeness, the completeness, the mystery of life itself eludes us. Modern society ignores the wisdom and spiritual connection with nature personified in indigenous cultures, preferring to wear the blinders of a mechanical and isolated approach to the world. Instead of understanding science as one way of viewing nature, we righteously insist it is the only way.

Today many people work to change these perceptions. Yet, as much as we would like to believe ourselves the vanguard of a new age, there is really nothing new at all about the philosophy which will be necessary to our survival: We have always belonged to the earth. The earth does not belong to us.

For centuries in North America, the indigenous peoples have been trying to impart that message to the newcomers.

The traditional native perception of the universe was one of wholeness, of belonging. The spirit of all life was contained in all things (animate as well as inanimate), and thus all things were sacred. To the Lakota, humans were simply "the sacred two-legged creatures," not in any way superior to "the sacred four-legged creatures," "the sacred winged creatures," the "sacred swimming creatures," or even rocks —"the silent, patient sacred ones."

In Haida legend, when the first humans came out of the sea, they were immortal — they could live forever. But a tiny wren, who liked to sing near grave sites, complained: "Where will I call if people live forever?" Today Haidas are mortal, like the rest of us, so the wren has a place to sing.

How different these philosophies and mythologies are from Western traditions, where humans are seen to have dominion over all creatures, where they follow an edict to go forth, and be fruitful, and multiply upon the earth, and subdue it.

When Europeans first came to the Western Hemisphere they believed themselves to be more civilized and knowledgeable, superior in every way to the original inhabitants they encountered. The audacity of that presumption is, in many ways, still with us today. They were so convinced of their superiority that it only made sense to give the natives the benefits of their religions, educational systems, political and social institutions. They baptized entire nations. They established Indian residential schools, where barefoot native youth were taken from their villages, forced into shoes, and reprogrammed in European ways. They punished native students for speaking their own language, imprisoned native leaders for pursuing their traditions, and forcibly removed the peoples from their homelands so that their lands could be turned over to white settlers and resources could be more reliably extracted.

Today many native people are faced with poverty, chronic unemployment, low life expectancy, high infant mortality, poor education levels, alcohol and drug abuse, and high suicide rates. As Hayden Burgess (president of the World Council of Indigenous Peoples) said:

"The cultural respect other societies accord indigenous cultures is a mirror of the advancement or regression of their own. We are all members of a large human family. Disregard for one member only results in disintegration of the family itself. By uplifting the rights of each member, we uplift the whole."

Rediscovery strives to uplift the whole: to help others open their minds and hearts in order to learn from indigenous peoples the world

Through wilderness, Rediscovery brings people in touch with the land, their cultural roots, and themselves. Traditional dancer in the Stein Valley.

Young traditional dancer.

over. It acknowledges that native pathways (lifestyles, value systems, and traditions) are as likely to hold a key to human survival as the trend toward western culture. As in the biological world, cultural diversity may be more than the "spice of life"; it may prove the secret to our survival.

It is interesting to note that a great number of modern pharmaceuticals are derived from rainforest plants first discovered by indigenous peoples. Much modern surgery depends on the bark of a South American liana vine, discovered by the Rayas Indians, who use it as an arrow poison. Further research in lianas has led to treatments for multiple sclerosis, Parkinson's disease, and other muscle disorders. Without them, such delicate operations as tonsillectomies and eye surgery would not be possible. For centuries malaria killed millions of people annually, yet the Indians on the Andean rainforest used the bark of the cinchona tree to cure it. It took three centuries, from the time the Amazon Indians first treated a Jesuit priest with fever bark in 1633, before Europeans accepted this tribal cure.

It is not only native knowledge of the land that directly benefits the rest of humanity, but native treatment of the land. Sustainable development in its truest form was the guiding principle of indigenous cultures

25

long before it became a coined term by a United Nations commission and a blueprint for global survival. One of the founders of Heiltsuk Rediscovery, Frank Brown, speaks of this guiding principle: "Rediscovery's foundation is based on indigenous cultures' harmonious relationship with the environment. These values are a gift, not to be taken lightly, but are shared in the hopes that they will be used as guidance in this time of unconscionable resource exploitation. This is necessary to ensure our existence in this world."

Rediscovery must not be confused with an attempt to turn back the clock — to return to some romanticized ideal of the past, even if for a moment that were possible. Rediscovery holds onto the present, the strengths and values which native cultures still embody: the strong ties of extended family; respect, love, and caring for the elders; the sacredness of sharing; and, above all, an intimacy and spiritual connection with the earth.

In many respects Rediscovery reverses the process of the Indian residential school. Through wilderness, it brings people back in touch with the land, their cultural roots, and, most of all, themselves. The non-natives who take part in Rediscovery benefit from an experience from which they are many generations removed. They share in the beauty and bounty of lands held in sacred trust — ancient village sites and campsites — often the least-disturbed camp locations to be found.

By pursuing pathways to cross-cultural understanding, Rediscovery programs everywhere may help to nurture a peaceful and mutually beneficial resolution of long-standing injustice. As Lester B. Pearson once said: "How can there be peace in the world if people don't understand one another; and how can they understand one another if they don't know each other."

With more than five billion people now testing the limits of global resources, and with mutually assured destruction well within our species capability, it is time for different nations and different cultures to come together in *knowing* and *understanding*. This coming together must not imply a steady homogenizing into one dominant culture, but should rather encourage diversity. We must learn to accept, respect, and even cherish our cultural differences. Simon Lucas, Nuu Chah Nulth elder, has said: "Without our differences we can never know the meaning of understanding."

CHAPTER 2
THE REDISCOVERY MODEL

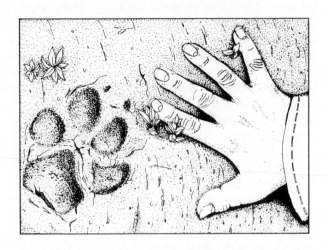

Rediscovery camps are initiated from within a community, usually by a group of people who decide they'd like to do something positive for the young people. The reasons for this decision vary: some want to introduce their children to traditional seasonal hunting and fishing camps and at the same time combat the feeling of boredom that many teenagers experience in isolated villages; others may want to pool the resources of several small towns to challenge their teenagers in a rugged wilderness rafting expedition, thus increasing their appreciation for the skills of their ancestors who travelled the same waterways. Still others want a vehicle that can help address some of the pressing social problems in their community. No matter what the reason, the underlying intent is to provide a cultural outdoor experience for local youth, and to let them know that somebody cares.

Often a community that wants to begin a youth camp invites a resource person from Rediscovery International Foundation to share ideas with them. During the past ten years, Rediscovery staff, with the advice of native elders, have tried many different activities and approaches, finding out what the participants need and like. Through this process emerged the following fourteen key elements of the Rediscovery Model.

Homeland, Heartland

In keeping with native traditions, contact with the land is the most important aspect of Rediscovery. All benefits and personal accomplishments are ultimately linked to this relationship. The participants are gently encouraged to notice their surroundings, and to become involved in the world around them. No one is ever forced to spend time alone in the wilderness. No one is ever coerced into appreciating a sunset or a star-filled night sky. But considering the settings of the camps — alpine meadows, desert dunes, and sandy Pacific beaches — the influence of the natural world is ever-present.

Fifteen-year-old Willie Dubroy wrote about his experience on Stein Rediscovery, capturing his response to the Stein Valley as he hiked and camped in it: "We took off, next destination, Iceberg Lake. Again we climbed — up, up, up, till we got to the top and over a rise. Then, WOW! There was Arrowhead Lake, the first alpine lake we had come to, aqua-blue, crystal clear and cool. We sat and rested there, after the hill and, looking around us, we realized that now we were definitely in the alpine. We pressed on, stopping to bathe in an un-named icy lake till finally we got to Iceberg Lake. Great!"

A few days later the group begins to hike down from the alpine, and Willie continues, "We began descending towards Stein Lake. We were going down a north slope to the valley, running along, when Maynard stopped and said, 'shaggymanes!' — pointing to a bunch growing beside the trail. We all got out our knives and started to look for things to carry the mushrooms in. Soon we got to the log jam across the mouth of the Stein and crossed to the other side where we proceeded to fry shaggymanes for our lunch (sure beats Ichiban!).

"After lunch, we all carried on down the river toward the first cable crossing where we would spend the night. We were in a forest of fir trees, so large that when you were among them, they made you feel very small and meaningless in comparison. We walked through these trees for hours by the river until we got to the cable crossing, loaded our stuff in, crossed the river, piled out and made camp."

When they reached base camp, the group stayed there for eight days, one of which was reserved for Solo, twenty-four hours alone. Willie describes the base camp site and his Solo: "Cottonwood Creek Falls, about fifteen minutes from base camp is one of the most beautiful places I've ever been, with high, high cliffs towering above a pool at the bottom of the falls, in which one could see trout swimming about. We'd dive into the pool from the cliff sides. Was it ever cold!

"My solo spot was on the banks of Cottonwood Creek. I sat there by myself for a while and watched the water. Then I made my bed in the duff and sand, covering it with fir boughs and laying out my sleeping bag on top of them.

"At daybreak, I awoke just in time to see two deer amble through my camp and get a drink, only to turn about and walk back through my camp. I got up and lit my fire, went for a swim, ate the rest of my raw potato and realized, that I was, in spite of the conditions, having the time of my life."

It was the Stein Valley itself, the creeks, trees, and lakes, that inspired Willie and gave him the time of his life. Nature helped him learn about himself, and gain confidence in his abilities. Similar influences were working on another Rediscovery participant, Dana Nyeholt, when she was alone at her Spirit Spot with a pencil and paper to record her impressions on the shores of Haida Gwaii:

Rocks are jagged
Seagulls soar
Not much can be heard
Over the ocean's roar
Sunlight rays shining on me
it just seems heavenly
an island across a bridge of water
waves below moving back
and forth like a teeter totter
the sunlight leaves temporarily
What's the matter did I do something
wrong. I lay back and listen
to the water's song
this is the way it should
sometimes be
just Mother Nature with me.

That is the way it should sometimes be. People alone with nature; reacting to its changes, its beauty. On Rediscovery, the wilderness is homeland, not frontier. It is the place from which sustenance is taken carefully, natural resources treated with the knowledge that future generations will also depend on the earth. Instead of reacting with a fortress mentality to wilderness, creating barricades, and destroying anything unfamiliar or wild, staff and participants try to live with and have respect for other living things.

Living From The Land

On Rediscovery, lunch may begin at dawn, with early risers taking advantage of a low tide to search for octopus. They must find the octopus lair, pry the eight-armed creature from its hiding place, kill, gut, clean, tenderize, and finally cook and serve their catch. Lunch may resemble a hot dog (an octopus arm in a bun) but the whole relationship with the creature being consumed and its connection to its environment could not be more pronounced. There is a saying on the coast that "when the tide goes out, the table is set." Halibut, cod, salmon, trout, abalone, mussels, clams, oysters, crab, rabbit, porcupine, venison, wild greens and berries are all eaten in their proper setting. There is one simple but effective rule governing their use: if you kill it, you eat it and fully utilize it. A deer will provide the camp with fresh meat for days, jerky for backpack expeditions, antlers and hoofs for rattles and regalia, and a hide for clothing or a skin drum. Following the dictates of traditional native use, the spirit of the animal is shown respect.

It is important to point out here, lest the wrong impression be given, that food gathering must be governed by principles of conservation and stewardship. This doesn't necessarily come naturally to children and sometimes must be emphasized. On Haida Gwaii, where deer were artificially introduced, have no predators, and suffer from overpopulation, it is far more ecologically sound to consume one of those animals than to ship in beef fattened in some feedlot hundreds of miles away.

In a world where so many urban youth have never seen the animal that fills their milk carton or the space between their Big Mac buns, it is a revelation for them to be involved directly in that most ancient human pursuit — food procurement. Even many rural youth may never have caught a fish, dug a clam, snared a rabbit, or planted, maintained, and harvested a garden.

HAIDA GWAII REDISCOVERY
FEAST MENU
Fried devilfish
Clam cabbage rolls
Stuffed mussels
Halibut Lepas
Barbequed salmon
Sweet and sour venison ribs
Fresh garden cole slaw
Bannock
Huckleberry/rhubarb pie

REDISCOVERY FOUR CORNERS
FEAST MENU
Fresh Rocky Mountain Trout
Elk Stew
Hot corn tamales
Pit-roasted Indian corn on the cob
Fresh garden and wild green salad
Rice with roasted piñon nuts
Wildberry cobbler

Extended Family

By keeping the number of participants small, eleven to sixteen per session, there is always a sense of family intimacy, and a good ratio of staff to youngsters for guidance and counselling. Each group includes boys and girls of many ages, ranging from eight to eighteen years old, native and non-native youth from diverse socio-economic backgrounds, creating a social microcosm of the local community. Within this extended family, space is reserved for elders and two to three youngsters from any part of the world.

Just as with any functional family, everyone prepares and eats meals together. Chores like dishwashing, woodcutting, and outhouse cleaning are shared by all. Staff can never require a youngster to do any chore that they do not take part in themselves. Staff also participate in the morning run and swim. If there are problems between any members of the group, time is taken to discuss and resolve them, either one-on-one or around the table or campfire.

Often elders bring their grandchildren and great-grandchildren, or volunteer cooks bring their young children out to camp. These very young children complete the family feeling. Participants who need to relax and take a break from others their age will take time out to play, build sandcastles, tell stories, or just have a tickle fight with the toddlers.

The only members of the family that don't fit in at Rediscovery camps are domestic pets. In the wilderness environment, pets can be disruptive: dogs chase deer, cats stalk wild birds, goats destroy natural vegetation, and chickens lure falcons and eagles on the hunt.

Elders

Native elders naturally assume the respected head position of a Rediscovery extended family. The original organizers felt that the elders would benefit the program most through their songs, stories, crafts, and

When the tide goes out the table is set — a non-native and Haida boy gather blue mussels for dinner.

Senior Guide and Rediscovery participant skin an octopus on Haida Gwaii Rediscovery.

skills. In addition to this, the elders have proven to be the program's most effective counsellors, transcending any generation gap between themselves and the coolest of teenagers.

Youth at odds with themselves, and adolescents generally, may tend to feel threatened by authority figures: parents, teachers, coaches, probation officers, and camp staff. The elders, perhaps because of their age and compassion, are more approachable. They appear as loving and caring grandparents — which is exactly what they are.

Many native elders concede that they cannot compete with television, video arcades, pool halls, or other town distractions. A drum song or traditional legend may appear dull and old-fashioned to a youngster hooked on the electronic wizardry of a rock video. But remove that same youngster from the distraction, and set him or her beside a wilderness campfire, and an elder now has a totally captive audience. The firelight works its magic, the uncommon darkness triggers the imagination, and the voice of the elder has a power no television saga could ever convey, forging a living link with the past. The elders feel useful, and the new respect and bond bridging the generations often carries back into the home community.

Cultural Context

Elders also advise the community members planning a Rediscovery as to locations suitable for base camps and routes for expeditions. Sites may be near ancient abandoned villages or hunting grounds, places that once sustained people and have the ability to do so again, places that hold special significance for local native people as the ground upon which their ancestors walked for hundreds, even thousands, of years. The campsites, rich in wildlife, are located far from the distractions of town and are untouched by logging, mining, or other development. The influence of a particular place upon the camp is never underestimated.

A traditional cedar bighouse graces the shores of Goose Island on Heiltsuk Rediscovery. Plains Indian tipis recall the ancient Ute occupation of southern Colorado at Rediscovery Four Corners. Interior Salish pit houses are being constructed at Stein Rediscovery in central British Columbia, and Polynesian pili-grass-thatched dwellings will bring authenticity to Rediscovery Hawaii. Every Rediscovery site reflects a distinct culture with its unique architecture, customs, traditions, language, skills, and spiritual focus. The settings and the facilities become powerful statements of the world view of the inhabitants.

Authenticity

To date, all Rediscovery camps have been based on native North American cultures and organized by native communities. Native people use the camps to further the ongoing education of native youth about their heritage. The majority of staff, elders, and resource people are native North Americans. The dances, songs, legends, and traditions they share are authentic, many originating from their ancestors, some newly created. The Wunskaw Wilderness Camp in northeastern Alberta gives children their first chance to go into a ceremonial sweat lodge. After attending Wunskaw, thirteen-year-old Derek Martin from Anzac, Alberta, said, "It helps me to think like an Indian to understand Indian culture." Native children who have been raised by non-native foster parents often join a Rediscovery session to experience that contact with their culture.

Indigenous people worldwide have sent requests for more information about Rediscovery. If they decide to develop a similar experience for their youth, they will share the same natural advantage of native North Americans, their long-standing connection with their land and countries. For immigrant cultures, such as the European descendants in North America, a rediscovery of their ancient traditions would be more difficult, having had a comparatively short history on this continent and without the same connection to the place. Yet the Rediscovery approach has universal applications. Youth everywhere need to spend time outside under the open sky, to discover more about themselves, their fellow humans, and the non-humans with whom they share this planet. Cultural authenticity is a guiding principle in Rediscovery camps but not their sole reason for being.

Cross-Cultural Understanding

Rediscovery brings together people from many different racial backgrounds, people who might otherwise never talk to each other, much less share the same tent or dinner table. At Rediscovery they live in an isolated wilderness environment in which they are interdependent. Racist attitudes thrive on ignorance: if one doesn't personally know someone from a different race, then it's easier to believe in stereotypes. But when people from different races have the opportunity to talk to one another, to work and play together, then inevitably they begin to learn about each other's lives and cultures.

If racial tension surfaces on a Rediscovery session, the staff never look away and pretend it isn't happening. The staff members themselves are usually from many different cultures and act as role models in co-

Shoshone and Arapahoe elders assume the respected head position of a Wind River Rediscovery extended family.

operation. Many activities on Rediscovery are designed to stimulate cross-cultural sharing and erase stereotypes. If prejudices continue, one-on-one talks are encouraged, or the individual concerned may find himself or herself sharing the same two-person kayak with a member of the other race for a week. New tolerances and even friendships sometimes begin in this way. Here is what one woman, Jenny C., wrote about her experience on Haida Gwaii Rediscovery:

"From the tradition of passing the eagle feather, I learned something quite unexpected and very important. During the first few times the feather was passed, I became aware that my impulse was to fill up the silences while people searched for words. I wanted to put words in their mouths or make bantering jokes when they hesitated. Partly this is a personal response. I have always enjoyed eloquence and the richness of words. But I also think this is a response which is typical of white society. We would rather tell than listen, and we are nervous with silence.

"I realize that I had listened to people without hearing them. My mind was racing ahead, searching for words. I was missing the silences and the important words which came out of them. One of the greatest treasures Rediscovery has given me is the new awareness of listening

Haida elders and youth prepare salmon and stick bannock around the campfire.

and respect for silence."

The potential for self-growth through understanding other cultures grows as each new community forms a Rediscovery. Rediscovery camps provide a meeting ground for people from distant areas. An exchange could take place between a young person from the Stein Rediscovery and the Four Corners Rediscovery in Colorado. In this way a person from an Interior Salish background would learn about Pueblo, Ute, or Navajo culture, and vice versa.

Flexible Schedule

Two-week sessions for teens and ten-day sessions for pre-teens have proven the optimum time frames for the Rediscovery experience. Most camps are so isolated that participants get homesick during longer stays. Conversely, short camp sessions do not allow time for the discoveries which can take place within oneself, between cultures, and intimately with nature.

A day at a Rediscovery camp is full of activities: meals, morning run and swim, chores, food gathering, sports, games, outdoor and cultural workshops, hikes, quiet time alone, free time, and evening campfire.

The main events of any two weeks are usually an expedition, a Solo/Vision Quest, and a Feast and Ceremony Night. Although these are the basic activities, each Rediscovery adapts them to the natural setting, the local culture, the preferences and ages of the children, the particular skills that the elders plan to share, and many other considerations specific to their camp.

Oftentimes natural circumstances dictate the schedule. High tide means no clam digging. A rainstorm means staying near base camp. Late sunsets in the northern summer sometimes mean that the group doesn't start gathering around the campfire until 10:30 p.m., and often the songs and storytelling go on until 1:30 a.m. The next morning everyone gets to sleep in before the run and swim.

There is no order as to when or how any activities should be done. Stein Rediscovery groups hike for three days through a high mountain pass to reach the Stein River base camp, where they have workshops and eight days of activities, Solo, and Ceremony before hiking out another three days to Lytton. Chako Kunamokst Rediscovery has canoe trips down the Dean Channel to traditional Nuxalk sites. The entire trip is an expedition, with stops for food gathering and a Solo along the way, while Ceremony happens back at the Kumsquit base camp.

The secret to a successful experience is knowing when to let go of the schedule. If a leader has planned a nature activity, but can't get the group's interest because they're too busy swimming and playing in the river, then the leader might put on his or her bathing suit and join them in the water. If the expedition group is aiming for a certain destination and is delayed due to berry picking and fossil hunting, then a closer spot becomes the destination. Ultimately the schedule of activities is adaptable, flexible, at times non-existent, at other times non-stop.

Sharing, Speaking Out

Many activities have no other aim than to encourage children to share their feelings. Eagle feathers, wooden staffs, crystals, and other special objects are passed from person to person around the campfire; only the person holding the "talking" object can speak. Paper, pencils, felt pens, and paints are available for Spirit Spot and Solo, times when participants spend time alone with nature. Often poems written at these times are read out at dinnertime, or artwork is displayed for everyone to see. Participants also share and express themselves through dance, song, play, and storytelling.

Personal sharing of problems and true-life stories often happens naturally under circumstances that would be difficult to duplicate in a principal or school counsellor's office. One Rediscovery staff member says he has the best heart-to-heart discussions with participants who volunteer to help in the garden after dinner. Because both people are busy harvesting, planting, or weeding, there's no pressure for either to speak. If they wish to talk they can, all the while keeping their hands busy. During every session each participant draws the name of a staff member to be their big brother or big sister, someone who will be available for long walks and talks. Staff members are trained in peer-counselling skills, and junior guides can often best understand what someone close to their own age is going through. All this doesn't take away from the role of elders, the most effective counsellors, who use kindness, a grandparent's love, and a good listening ear as their tools.

Nature acts as a catalyst for self-expression, and is the ideal place to share thoughts with others. Once a rapport has been established between people, and a young person realizes that what he or she feels is important, that sense of self-worth and trust in others will carry back to the community. If they are ever in serious need, hopefully they will remember there are people who care and who will listen.

Sharing also includes providing a shoulder to cry on, a "way-to-go" high-five hand slap, a pat on the back, or a hug of comfort. Staff try to act as role models, providing examples of what is appropriate physical contact between friends. For children who have been physically abused in the past, a hug that has no ulterior motive besides friendship is a reassuring thing.

Personal Achievement

The following two Rediscovery soloists had different experiences when they spent their twenty-four hours alone, but they both overcame obstacles: one physical, building a fire with two matches; the other mental, staying out on the solo without a fire after the matches were gone. Achievements, small and large, do not slip by unnoticed on Rediscovery.

"Ya Hoo! I got my fire started on my two matches. It sure feels good! It was blowing like crazy and then my hair got all singed, but who cares? I have heat!!! I feel I'm one of the luckiest people in the whole world to be out here in the wilderness, to be by myself, to have the roar of the wind and the screech of the eagles above me...." — Christine MacDonald, Rediscovery participant

Haida longhouses bring cultural authenticity to Haida Gwaii Rediscovery (above), while a log cabin, food cache, and tipis provide Stein Rediscovery's facilities (below).

Like a well-functioning family, everyone shares in Rediscovery camp chores. (Although sometimes it's only in a fun way.)

"This is freaky with no fire, no more matches, freaky noises. Goghits everywhere ready to jump me. Some fun." — Theodore Noddin, Rediscovery participant

The soloists are honoured at the final ceremony fire, as are all participants for individual accomplishments. The group chooses one person to be honoured, the one who has helped others the most and who has achieved the greatest personal gains. Perhaps they select the youngest in the group, who cheerfully kept pace with everyone else on a four-day hike, or the person who grumbled at first about having to paddle thirty-five miles but who ended up paddling the hardest. Achievements are all measured relative to the attitudes and abilities each person had when they arrived at Rediscovery and how "far" they have come by the final day. Staff also recognizes achievement on a daily basis, using the dinner meal as a time to recount who chopped the wood for the evening's campfire, who helped the cook prepare the day's meals, or who was first to spot the bear wandering close to camp.

Many teenagers feel that the only recognition they receive from adults is in the form of reprimand: poor grades in school, detentions for disrupting classes, grounded for talking back. Sometimes negative acts, such as vandalism and theft, result in more serious *recognition*: probation and community service hours.

When the Attorney General of B.C. and the Solicitor General of Canada released funds for the first Rediscovery, one of their main concerns was the high juvenile crime rate in one of the communities on Haida Gwaii. (Out of a population of 1,500, more than fifty young people were on probation.) Rediscovery is designed as a wilderness adventure, not a corrections camp. Everyone who participates does so because they want to, not because they have to as punishment. As with any wilderness adventure, milestones are encountered: having to wash clothes in a bucket or wading across an icy mountain river. As the participants surpass each milestone, they receive recognition for their accomplishments. According to the Solicitor General, in his telegram on Rediscovery's tenth anniversary, this method is working:

"I am delighted to see that Rediscovery Society is celebrating its tenth anniversary today. This is an organization that has favourably altered the lives of its many local participants over the years ... and enriched the lives of Masset's people. The off-shoot programs which have mushroomed across B.C. as well as abroad are a remarkable example of how quickly a good and working idea can spread. As Solicitor General of Canada, I am grateful for having had an opportunity to play a small role in this important program. I wish you all the very best and continued success." — James Kelleher, Solicitor General of Canada

Healthy Living

Each morning at Rediscovery, everyone is encouraged to stretch, run, and take an invigorating bath in a cold creek, lake, or ocean — all before breakfast. Breakfast includes fresh foods, possibly salal-berry pancakes, abalone and eggs, or huckleberry porridge. There's no place to buy pop, potato chips, or chocolate bars. The air is clean. The drinking water is pure, from a well or mountain creek. This might seem like too ideal a picture — well, maybe the occasional sweet snack sneaks into the menu — but for the most part, the days are full of hiking, swimming, and backpacking, and a healthy diet of gathered and home-grown foods. This type of outdoor experience naturally improves health, physical fitness, and general well-being.

All Rediscovery camps provide an alcohol- and drug-free environment. This guideline applies to both staff and participants. For some young people this may be the first time in their lives they are not exposed to these substances or people under their influence. Although those inclined to indulge in alcohol and drugs may continue to do so after they leave Rediscovery, two weeks is enough time for a teenager to experience a different lifestyle and to learn that it's possible to have a good time with friends without alcohol and drugs. More and more Rediscovery camps are also encouraging cigarette-free environments.

Healthy living also includes following common-sense safety rules. All boaters must wear life jackets and practise emergency procedures in case of capsizing. All leaders are trained in first aid, carry first-aid kits, and, depending on how far the area is from a town, they may carry radiophones. Participants who cut wood wear heavy boots and pants. Those who carve learn proper ways to handle carving tools. Those who take part in hunts are trained in gun safety and allowed to accompany an experienced guide. Strict rules are followed in potentially dangerous situations and with dangerous tools, which fosters a respect in the participants for the safety of their own lives and those of others.

Leadership Skills

Staff are trained in a variety of areas: navigation, map reading, compass work, first aid, native technologies, peer counselling, bush survival, and many other leadership skills. Good leaders are not macho or bossy; instead they have knowledge, courage, and a sensitivity to the

Participants on Haida Gwaii Rediscovery share in the planning of a one-hundred-kilometre kayak expedition.

needs of all the members of the group. Both girls and boys are equally encouraged to be leaders. To date, fifty local youth have received training as junior and senior guides on the Haida Gwaii Rediscovery. Very often a youngster will come on the program as a pre-teen, return a few years later for the teen program, then apply to become a junior guide. Good performance as a junior guide results in promotion to senior guide status and opens the way to camp supervisor or program director positions. As Alice Martin, director of Wunskaw Wilderness Camp, says, "Our hope is that the older children will in turn be the leaders and organizers in these programs."

The Haidas have started up their own wilderness guiding company, the Haida Gwaii Watchmen. The Watchmen perform the dual function of village site guardians and commercial tour operators in Gwaii Haanas — South Moresby. Young people who have acquired leadership skills through their Rediscovery experience have an added advantage when they apply to be a Haida Gwaii Watchmen Guide. Adventure tourism is the fastest-growing sector of tourism, which is the fastest-growing industry in the world. Wilderness leadership skills are becoming highly employable skills.

The Journey to Ninstints ends at the UNESCO World Heritage Site, the ancient Haida village of Ninstints.

Further Education

Rediscovery leaders have one natural advantage over schoolteachers: the outdoor setting. Students who become bored sitting in a classroom all day get excited exploring a tide pool or sleeping overnight on a midden in a cave that native people have slept in for thousands of years. There's a great difference between reading about a marmot in a textbook and whistling at one a few feet away.

Environmental and cultural learning is taught using immersion, observation, exploration with all senses, and finally appreciation. For example, marine biology might be taught in the following ways: the participants explore a tide pool with their fingers, feeling what is slimy, sticky, or sharp; they observe the creatures in the pool, maybe using diving masks to watch two hermit crabs battle over a new shell home; then they draw a picture of the tide pool and all the creatures they can see in it, linking together what eats what; finally they play an active game, all taking on the roles of different tide pool dwellers. The "lesson" might continue with the group walking to a sandy beach to compare what living things they find there, or if it's a rainy day they could play Beach-Life Bingo indoors. To continue the learning the next day, they may go on an octopus hunt with an elder. There's also usually a small library of books available on related subjects to refer to or simply look at the pictures.

Judith Kerr, a Masset, B.C., youth counsellor, speaks of her visit to Rediscovery: "This last year I was struck more than ever with the value of the education the young participants were receiving, and at how well designed the workshops were. Whether you were forty or five, the workshops captured your imagination and led you through a true experience in education."

A Rediscovery workshop is never too rigid not to be interrupted or forgotten if something more interesting turns up. The cry, "Hey, look at this over here," means that the leader calls time-out in the workshop and everyone comes over to have a look. Time that was scheduled for workshops may be better spent observing a spider wrapping a fly, an army of ants carrying away some lunch crumbs, or a black bear rummaging in the berry bushes.

These workshops and outdoor experiences are not meant to replace a more formal education, simply to add to and enhance it. Often students who have become discouraged or have dropped out of school may get excited about learning and begin to pursue formal education again.

Follow-Up

All too often, positive changes in a Rediscovery participant erode when that youngster returns to a home or school life that is falling apart. Ideally, a year-round program could provide opportunities for wilderness adventures after school, on weekends, and on school holidays. The staff, especially the Junior Guides, could be hired as peer counsellors in the schools, and there could be youth centres run by youth in the communities. In Bella Coola, the Nuxalk Youth Council, together with Chako Kunamokst Rediscovery, organize year-round events such as ski trips to lodges, youth conferences, and trips to other communities. Having been exposed to the wilderness, many teenagers find their way back to the land — camping with their friends, or getting food with their families. Rediscovery becomes an important stepping stone in this process.

The Haida elders also recognize the need for effective follow-up and ongoing counselling after participants return home. To meet this need in the community of Masset, elders open their homes to young people during the winter months, treating the children as their own. In their kitchens and living rooms, they may teach bark basketry, button blanket making, and dance. Being part of a Haida dance group is prestigious amongst the young, who practise regularly in the home of one of the chiefs. Other communities also have traditional dance groups that hold practices and sometimes go on tour. More opportunities for cross-cultural exchanges between distant places would give youth a chance to learn about other cultures, and to put their home community into perspective.

Other aspects of follow-up are in the planning and pilot stages, such as Adult and Family Rediscovery sessions. Adults benefit from and enjoy a chance to make contact with the land as much as young people. Entire families could escape from the pressures of day-to-day life, and get to know each other and the wilderness a little better. At present, much development is needed for follow-up programs, but there's no shortage of good community-generated ideas, and it's only a matter of time before these ideas become reality.

Rediscovery recognizes that not all knowledge is taught in the same school.

PART II

REDISCOVERING

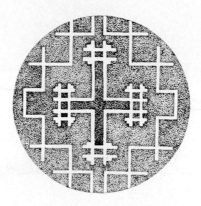

Civilized people depend too much on man-made printed pages. I turn to the Great Spirit's book which is the whole of creation. You can read a big part of that book if you study nature. You know, if you take all your books, lay them out under the sun, and let the snow and rain and insects work on them for a while, there will be nothing left. But the Great Spirit provided you and me with an opportunity for study in nature's university, the forests, the rivers, the mountains, and the animals which include us.

— Tatanga Mani (Stoney Indian)

CHAPTER 1
THE WORLD WITHIN

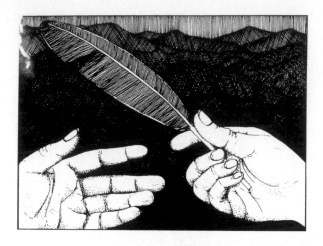

Thirty young eyes reflect the glow of firelight as an eagle feather passes clockwise from person to person around the campfire circle. It is a "Talking Feather," and only the person holding it may speak. All are encouraged to speak truthfully from their hearts.

"We all have a lot of growing to do during our next two weeks together," the staff member holding the feather tells the campers. "If there comes a time when we have clearly matured in our relationship with one another, we will exchange this immature eagle feather for an adult one." The next several youngsters to hold the feather speak lightly of the things they experienced their first day in camp and the good time they're having. But now the feather passes to a boy who is more solemn. There is a long silence, and suddenly he says: "I don't think I look funny, I don't think my nose is too long. I don't think I'm a wimp and I'm tired of being picked on!" The boy falls silent as quickly as he has exploded. He strokes the feather of the young eagle for a long time before passing it to his left. There is another long silence, throat clearing, and in an unsteady voice the next boy has the courage to say, "I think we all owe David an apology. I know I do. A wimp wouldn't stand up like that." The eagle feather passes completely around the circle again, each child expressing their feelings about ridicule and being the object of ridicule.

A growing bond is forming. It is only the first night of camp and an uncommon occurrence, but before the fire has died to embers an adult eagle feather has replaced the immature one.

Self-discovery receives much of the early focus of every Rediscovery session. Youth in crisis and at risk have very special needs that differ markedly from normal youngsters. To address these needs, government and private foundations tend to establish special agencies and institutions to address each of these problem areas. Unfortunately, these systems all too often fail in their approach, because the only peer role models present are other problem youth.

Juvenile offenders, incarcerated or sentenced to a corrections camp, often come away from the experience more streetwise and inclined to a life of crime. Their associations become limited strictly to other kids in trouble with the law. At Rediscovery camps, troubled youngsters have an opportunity to compare their behaviour to a greater cross-section of their peers. Self-discovery becomes an ongoing process — from the moment they enter camp to long after they leave.

BONDING

The first minutes of a Rediscovery session, or any group-encounter session, are critical for overcoming initial shyness, inhibitions, and fears, and binding together a workable cohesive unit. The following activities have been successfully used for this purpose at Rediscovery summer camps and conference community workshops for more than a decade. These games and activities are for youth of all ages — pre-teens, teens, and adults alike. A good icebreaker involves touch, silliness, fun, and laughter. By working together toward a common goal and learning to depend on one another, a bond of trust can be quickly built within a group.

Circle Greetings / Cinnamon Roll

Circle Greetings is an excellent introductory activity for a group at the very start of a session. Form a large circle with everyone holding hands and facing inward. A group leader welcomes everyone to their new, large family and begins introducing himself or herself by shaking hands with the person to the left. The first person he or she shakes hands with immediately follows the leader doing the same. Everyone continues shaking hands around the circle until each person has met every other. Eventually everyone returns to the spot where he or she began.

With everyone again holding hands, the group leader now says,

The first minutes of a Rediscovery session are critical for overcoming initial shyness.

"Today is only our first day together so we only feel this close," raising held hands. "But by the end of our time together I'll bet we feel *this* close." The leader releases his or her right hand and immediately starts turning counterclockwise on the spot. A great human cinnamon roll begins to form with much shrieking and laughter. Once everyone is a part of the roll, the leader in the centre can shout, "Press the roll smaller!" The big squeeze will quickly break down any inhibitions anyone might have about touch activities.

Trust Fall / Lift Turn

Trust Fall/Lift Turn, a good follow-up to the Cinnamon Roll, requires groups of eight to ten. Each group forms a support unit for a volunteer who will close his or her eyes and fall backward into the waiting arms of their support team. Have the taller and stronger members of the support group in position to receive the shoulders, back, hips, and thighs of the volunteer. In one smooth movement, the volunteer is lifted skyward, so that all arms of the support team are fully extended. At this point the volunteer should be instructed to relax totally, open their eyes, throw out their arms, and greet the sky — a powerful experience on a

A good icebreaker binds the group together with touch, silliness, fun, and laughter.

starlit night. The group now slowly rotates their volunteer three times and returns them, feet first, gently to the earth. Others will immediately wish to follow, and eventually everyone in the group learns to trust, rely on, and support one another.

Human Knot

Use the same groups that just finished Trust Fall/Lift Turn, or groups of comparable size. Ask everyone to grasp someone else's hand in the group in an imaginative or creative way, i.e., behind the back, between the legs, or across the group. When all hands are clasped securely, tell the group they must now untie their human knot and form a circle without breaking a single handhold. The group dynamics of this activity can be hilarious. Two or more teams racing against one another to undo their knot adds to the fun.

Red Shoe, Blue Shoe, My Shoe, Whose Shoe

Sit everyone in a circle, and have each person remove the shoe on their right foot and throw it into a pile at the centre of the circle. Now totally mix the pile of shoes.

On a signal everyone grabs a shoe (other than their own) from the pile, puts it on, and returns to the spot where they were sitting. The instructor now demonstrates how each person is to rematch with their missing shoe.

When a person finds their right shoe on another's foot, they must match their left shoe beside it by putting their left leg between the legs of the person wearing their shoe. In this way everyone ultimately gets linked up. The challenge is in trying to walk in unison with another person's leg on each side of yours, while the people at the end of the line are searching for their match. Until shoe partners link up they can call for others still searching with the words: "Red shoe, blue shoe, who's got my shoe?"

Shed The Snake Skin

Form two single-file lines of participants, with all players facing the same direction. Be certain there is enough space behind each line to double its length, and that the floor or ground space is relatively clean to lie on. Instruct everyone in the line-up to spread their legs wide while standing, reach between them with their right hand, and grasp the left hand of the person behind them. Once the two teams are linked up, explain the procedure. The last person in line is to lie down. The line then shuffles backward until the next person can lie down. The object of the game is to get the entire line lying down without breaking the chain of hands and then back into their original standing positions by reversing the process. To do this successfully, everyone must move together cooperatively and lie closely with legs around the person in front. Have two teams race against each other for a competitive Shed the Snake Skin or one long line race against the clock for a fast-paced, non-competitive activity.

Ha, Ha, Ha!!!

For the ultimate in silliness, have everyone form a line by lying on their backs at right angles to one another with their heads resting on one another's stomachs. (The line will resemble a layout of dominoes.) The first person in line has to give a big belly laugh "Ha!" so that everyone can hear. The next person does the same, adding a laugh. "Ha! Ha!" The next person must laugh "Ha! Ha! Ha!", and so on down the line.

If anyone gets carried away and starts laughing more than their share of "Ha, Ha, Ha's," the game must start all over again. A thirtieth person in line will have quite a challenge getting out thirty belly laughs without an extra "Ha, Ha" or two.

Missing Link

This activity is fairly well known, but is so effective in getting the point across that it works well to close an icebreaking session. Form a large circle as perfectly round as possible, with everyone holding hands and facing inward. Now close the circle tightly so that all shoulders touch. Instruct everyone to turn to their right and put both hands on the shoulders of the person in front of them. Explain that on signal everyone will sit down on the chair provided by the lap of the person behind them. "Now slowly ease down into a sitting position and on the count of one-two-three, sit!" Everyone is amazed to see that the circle supports itself sitting as well as standing. This circle sit has been done effectively with hundreds of people at a time.

A group leader will now explain that together we can all support one another. "But what happens if someone is left out?" The leader quickly becomes the missing link by casting himself or herself out of the sitting circle. The domino effect of collapsing chairs is great fun, and hopefully brings the message home to all.

A group plays Ha, Ha, Ha!!! at Chako Kunamokst Rediscovery.

Group Picnic

Now that the group has interacted in a completely informal fashion, it is time to learn everyone's name. This often difficult task in a large group can be greatly simplified by association. Everyone sits in a circle while the leader explains that the group is about to go on a picnic. Each person brings a food starting with the same first letter as their name. The next person in the circle must give his or her name and food, as well as repeat the name and food of everyone before them: "My name is Peter and I'm bringing pickles, Sally's bringing soup, Jeff's bringing jam, and Dennis is bringing devilled eggs." The larger the group, the more frequently each name gets repeated. Three days into a session you may not be able to recall Margaret's name but you will not have forgotten that somehow she is associated with marshmallows.

Dox - En - Eye

An all-time favourite Haida game, now used on many Rediscovery programs, Dox-en-eye involves two teams constantly changing in size and composition but not really competitive at all. The game begins with two equal-sized teams sitting and facing each other about five to ten

Dox-En-Eye is played at Rediscovery Four Corners.

metres apart. One member from each team comes forward to compete for the Dox-en-eye stick, a straight stick one metre long. Decide who has first turn by using the old hand-over-hand (baseball-bat) method with the stick. The winner of the Dox-en-eye stick then returns to his or her team, sits down, and begins pounding the ground with the stick, shouting, "Dox-en-eye, Dox-en-eye, send us Shirley." The person named on the opposite team must immediately turn stone-faced, get up and slowly cross the clearing to take the stick away from the opposing team, and return to their seated position without smiling. The opposing team can do everything and anything short of actually touching the person to make them lose their composure. If the person called smiles or laughs, they immediately become a member of the team that called them. Another person is then called by the same team. If the person called gets the Dox-en-eye stick successfully back to the team from which they came, that team then does the calling. The game continues until everyone is on one team. There are no losers in Dox-en-eye, only winning smiles.

I Love You Darling

A favourite game with Chako Kunamokst Rediscovery in Bella Coola, I Love You Darling can get the entire group grinning. Everyone sits in a circle, and a volunteer approaches a person of their choice, sits playfully in their lap, and pleads: "I love you darling, so won't you please just smile?" This is repeated three times at close range: eye-to-eye contact, theatrical gestures, and silly voices are in order, but no tickling. The second party must remain expressionless and repeat three times, "I love you too darling, but I just can't smile." At the first sign of a grin, the person approached becomes 'it' and must find a new person to make smile. If by any chance the person pleading cannot make the object of their affection smile, they must continue seeking out new victims within the circle. Such situations are, needless to say, rare.

Pass A Clap

Another game which comes from Bella Coola requires split-second group timing and interaction: Pass a Clap can be played anywhere a group of people can stand in a circle. Face the circle inward, with everyone's feet planted shoulder-width apart. To play Pass a Clap properly one must be able to pivot the upper torso quickly. First, everyone needs to practise clapping their hands in unison with the person to their right and to their left. Once the timing has been perfected, the high-speed game can begin. A leader announces that a very hot clap is coming around the circle so move it quickly. It will take the clap a few revolutions of the circle to really start building up speed. Eventually the clap moves like a tangible object — a fireball of energy swirling around the circle. Now the leader introduces a new element — a second clap. Start this one when the first clap reaches halfway around the circle, and see which of the two claps catch up with the other. When back to only one clap, the leader can suddenly call out a name and hurl the clap across the circle to that person. Now the clap is totally unpredictable, it has a life of its own, anyone can pass it to anyone else as it races around the circle.

Two Truths And A Lie

A good campfire activity, Two Truths and a Lie helps the group learn a little more about each individual. The group sits in a circle, and the leader asks everyone to think of two statements about themselves which are true and one which is false. The leader may begin, "I have three brothers but no sisters. My favourite sport is hockey and I love peanut butter." The person to the speaker's left must guess which statement is the lie. As soon as the deceit is uncovered, the next person in the circle begins. This simple exercise helps overcome initial shyness and opens the doors to self-expression.

A What? A What? A What?

This exercise is pure fun and perfect for an evening of entertainment around the campfire. For the game to work properly, everyone must sit in a fairly uniform circle. A staff member introduces a natural object that the students have been learning about, such as a spruce branch. "This is a spruce tree branch," the staff member will say to the person sitting to his or her right. "A what?" the person being given the branch must ask. "A spruce branch," the staff member repeats as the branch is handed over.

The new holder of the branch now turns to the person on his or her right and repeats the same statement. "This is a spruce branch." When the second player asks "A what?", the first player must pass the same question back to the staff. "A what?" Only the staff member who initiated the game can answer the question: "A spruce branch!" Player number one now repeats "A spruce branch" to player number two. By the time player number three is involved it sounds something like this: "This is a spruce branch." "A what?" "A what?" "A what?" "A spruce branch." "A spruce branch." "A spruce branch." Simple enough, except that the game actually involves two different objects being passed in opposite directions around the circle at the same time. While a spruce branch passes to the right, a pine branch will follow the same procedure to the left. Needless to say, the spruce branch and pine branch become more than a little confusing as the two objects begin to cross paths at the end of the circle of players.

Invite those participants who believe themselves to be especially bright and clever to take up positions on the far end of the circle opposite the staff member, prior to starting the game. Almost without exception they will make a few major blunders, to everyone's amusement.

Do not let the simplicity of the game fool you: adults have much more trouble with it than children. The objects move very quickly with young people because the procedure is so clear and straightforward. There are really only three things that one can possibly say: 1) "This is a spruce branch (pine branch)"; 2) "A what?"; and 3) "A spruce branch (pine branch)." Adults tend to overrationalize and discuss unnecessarily. The two objects are supposed to be racing one another around the circle to see which makes it back to the beginning first. Interestingly enough, a direct and inverse relationship exists between the age and intelligence of the players and the time required to get the objects back to the beginning. To date, the record for the slowest completion of this game is held by a group of high-tech wizards from Silicon Valley, California.

Apart from the obvious fun and hilarity, this exercise serves to remind everyone of the need to not make situations overly complicated. There is also an environmental-education component with the objects being used. Hopefully, the players will never again mistake a spruce branch for a pine branch.

SHARING AND CARING

Group sharing is one of the most healing experiences for troubled youth and adults alike. Often participants reveal deeply repressed psychological traumas at these sessions. Youngsters should never be pressured to share their feelings; they should just be provided the opportunity. Self-expression has a remarkable ability to ease the pain of those in crisis. Caring for others, building self-esteem, sharing feelings and fears, and identifying with positive behavioural models are all important qualities of group sharing. The following activities, though simple, have been profoundly effective in helping people to open up, speak freely, understand their emotions, and feel better about themselves.

Talking Feather

Put a shy person in front of a group to speak, then watch their hands. Often the hands go into their pockets, up to fix their hair, over to wiggle a loose shirt button, and back into their pockets. But give the same person an object to hold while they speak and they can forget about what to do with their hands, concentrating more on what they want to say. On Rediscovery the object is endowed with power. "This is a talking feather," the leader tells the group around the fire on the first evening. "It is a very special feather because it will give you the power to speak. There are rules you must observe when holding this sacred feather. You and you alone may speak. You must speak from the heart and you must speak the truth. Always treat the feather with respect and pass it clockwise around the circle."

According to Haida elders, such a system was used for group sharing from time beyond memory. Chiefs still hold a talking stick when addressing a group. Not all native groups can use eagle feathers in this manner: to some the feather is so sacred that only a shaman may hold one. The Ute, Lakota, and Pueblo peoples on Colorado's Rediscovery Four Corners pass a crystal rather than an eagle feather. Any object can be imbued with "talking powers" once the group recognizes it as such. The more natural and culturally appropriate the object is, the greater the powers it will possess.

The policy at many Rediscovery camps is that if a crisis occurs in camp or an individual is seriously troubled, anyone can call for the feather to be passed. Whatever activity is under way at that time, be it a meal, a hike, group game, or workshop, will be stopped immediately. Nothing is more important than an individual needing to express himself or herself through the feather. Participants have never been known to abuse this privilege.

One extremely important lesson for group leaders, sometimes learned the hard way, is to respect a person's silence. Group leaders can get so caught up in facilitating that at times they are tempted to try helping a youngster who holds the feather but can't find words to speak. A Haida elder set us straight on that point: "A child's silence is as important a statement as any words spoken by any other child."

Begin with one "talking" object and progress to a similar (but older or larger) object during the course of the program to help the group mark their personal development and growth. For instance, replace an immature eagle feather with an adult eagle feather or a small crystal with a larger rock when the staff feels that the group has really matured together. By marking such a progression, everyone has the new responsibility of the more advanced behaviour or attitude toward each other. They can be reminded that they've all advanced to a higher level, should any temporarily regress.

Stoneribs — The Mythical Role Model

Perhaps no single Rediscovery technique works as well for influencing behaviour than the use of a mythical role model. Stoneribs, a central character in ancient Haida mythology, has become a living legend during the past decade on Haida Gwaii's Rediscovery.

According to legend, Stoneribs was not always the powerful person he came to be. As a young boy, often ridiculed for his weakness, he was known as Boneribs or Iceribs, and spent long periods alone in the forest and by the seashore in search of supernatural powers. That power came one day in the form of an enormous eagle, which dropped a shining copper-coloured halibut on the rock beside him. Thinking the villagers would at least regard him a good fisherman if he returned with the beautiful halibut, Boneribs immediately tried to gut the fish with his knife. But lightning struck and thunder rumbled when he tried to pierce the fish's belly. Suddenly the boy was overcome by a strange desire to crawl inside the huge halibut. Before he knew it, he was a halibut, and in this new-found form was able to battle and defeat Kostan, the giant crab that plagued the village harbour entrance, and Scannah, the dreaded five-finned killer whale that swamped Haida canoes. Returning to his village as Boneribs, the boy was welcomed as a hero and was bestowed the name of Stoneribs by the Chief. From that day on, Stoneribs travelled throughout the Islands, helping Haida perform tasks too great for mortal humans.

The potential of a role model that taught self-esteem, closeness to nature, pride in one's culture, and service to others was a strong determining factor in Rediscovery adopting the Stoneribs model at the program's inception in 1978. This had to be done with the consent of the Haida elders, as stories, names, and songs are all personal family property. Once the model was consented to, a remarkable tradition began.

At the first night's campfire on each Rediscovery session, the staff tell or act out the Stoneribs legend for the new participants. "We're all going to try to be like Stoneribs while we're here together these next few weeks," the staff explains. "We're going to discover new abilities we never knew we had; we're going to grow closer to the spirit of this land. We're going to come to know, understand, and respect the cultural differences between us and we're going to serve each other cheerfully. This is the spirit of Stoneribs, and you all have it within you."

Throughout the duration of the program, the model of Stoneribs is repeatedly called upon to help youngsters through various situations. On the last full day of the program, every person in camp has an opportunity to vote in a secret ballot for the participant they feel best lived up to the Stoneribs ideal. All voters are encouraged to give the reasons they choose that person. The group often honours one who has come the furthest in attaining Stoneribs qualities, rather than one who came to the program already possessing those traits. Although the Haida legend has Stoneribs as a boy, it is made clear to the group that the honour can just as easily be bestowed upon a girl. To reinforce this, the Haida elders made a special female Stoneribs costume, which many girls have had the honour to wear.

Stoneribs' power came in the form of a shining copper-coloured halibut.

The model of Stoneribs is repeatedly called upon to help youngsters through difficult situations — a Haida and non-native boy learn co-operation pitching a tent.

*In a dramatic torch-lit procession, the participant chosen as
Stoneribs is led by the staff to the ceremony fire.*

In a dramatic torch-lit procession, the staff leads Stoneribs to the final
night's ceremony fire. As in the legend, Stoneribs enters the fire circle
"dressed in a sacred manner," carrying a whale rib on one shoulder to
symbolize willingness to help others, a talking staff to symbolize
leadership, and a hemlock sash to symbolize closeness with nature and
overcoming fear of being alone in the woods. All the votes are read
before the group, and the ballots burnt on the ceremonial fire. Stoneribs
is acknowledged and presented with a gift made by the staff. "We have
paid special tribute to one here tonight," the program director announces, "but each of you in your own way have become like
Stoneribs." Each participant is then called forward by their hike leader,
who highlights all their special accomplishments before the group. They
too receive gifts. For some youngsters this marks the first time in their
lives they have received public recognition for positive traits.

The Stoneribs model originates from Haida culture and is perfectly
suited to Haida Gwaii's Rediscovery, but this model would not be
appropriate on another Rediscovery with a different cultural focus. The
"Mitlakla Spirit Warrior" role model utilized on Bella Bella's Heiltsuk
Rediscovery and the "Strong Heart Award" honouring Stoneribs-type

qualities at Rediscovery Four Corners in Colorado, show how culturally appropriate models can be employed on other programs.

Secret Friend

At the opening of a Rediscovery session every person in camp draws at random the name of another person in camp written on a folded piece of paper. Once everyone has selected their Secret Friend for the next two weeks, they are duty-bound to tell no one the identity of that person. Each day a special act is performed for one's special friend, or a gift secretly given. This is one of the most delightful ways to show you care about someone and in turn be cared for. For instance, a person might make up their friend's bed without them knowing, or deliver a poem, painting, or a bouquet of flowers, or a gentle shoulder massage via an anonymous messenger. These experiences happen to everyone in camp all the time and at the most unexpected times. During dinner a staff member might ask, "Did anyone notice anything their special friend did for them today?" A flood of responses usually follows, reminding anyone who still hasn't done something for their friend to do so before the day is out. A camp cook confessed that she was at a low point of weariness late in the day when suddenly a wilderness flower-gram arrived from her secret friend: "It gave me such a boost I felt like the day had just begun." On the final day of camp, everyone may want to guess who their Secret Friend has been, or they may just want to keep it a *special secret* all their life.

Big Brother / Big Sister

No matter how small or intimate camp might be, it is always possible for someone to feel slightly left out. To ensure that this doesn't happen on Rediscovery, every participant has a Big Brother or Big Sister. All the camp staff write their names on pieces of paper, which are folded and drawn from a basket by each youngster on the opening day of camp. (Some staff will necessarily have their names drawn more than once.) The Big Brother or Big Sister spends extra time with their Little Brother or Little Sister every day to see how he or she is feeling. They may go for walks together, share chores, or have a sunset Viewing Party. Sometimes very strong bonds form and the randomly selected brother or sister becomes the most effective counsellor for that child. This system also discourages any youngster trying to bully or pick on another, because there is always the Big Brother or Big Sister to contend with. Often this relationship will carry over back in the home community, where the Big Brother or Big Sister can offer an effective follow-up for counselling throughout the year.

Lovable And Capable

Lovable and Capable is effective role-play, especially for a group engaged in a lot of little "putdowns" of each other. The staff can fill some of the roles, but participant involvement will help the youngsters relate even more to the exercise. One person becomes the child always being "put down." He or she wears a paper sign (safety-pinned to the shirt or attached by a string behind the neck) which reads, "I am lovable and capable." The other characters include: father, mother, brother/sister, school teacher/coach (or camp staff), classmate (or fellow camper), and grandparent (or wise elder).

The role-play begins with a staff narrator describing how good the child feels about himself or herself when they wake up in the morning — a lovable and capable person — looking forward to a new day. The first putdown comes from the parents. "Why didn't you make your bed before breakfast? Your room is a mess. Comb your hair, it looks awful. Hurry, you're late for school, you're always late." With each little putdown the child tries to respond, but is never given the chance. He or she begins to tear little rips in the "lovable and capable" sign. A staff narrator leads the group through the story. At each encounter during the day the child becomes a more and more tattered individual. The role players will easily come up with putdowns that they've all heard before.

By the end of the day, the child's self-image has been largely destroyed. An elder, or grandparent, takes the dejected child aside, sits down, and lovingly asks what the problem is. As the child recounts the experience of the day, the elder offers comforting words and begins Scotch-taping the "lovable and capable" sign back together. The elder assures the child that things will be better tomorrow, gives the child the roll of Scotch tape, and then speaks to some of the characters involved in the putdowns, telling them to take a more positive approach.

Repeat the whole role-play for another make-believe day: this time with all the characters finding something positive to say. With each complimentary statement, the child tapes back together a little more of his or her self-image. By the end of the day, a "lovable and capable" child's dignity has been restored.

Story Stick

Almost every youngster loves scary stories around a campfire, but how

A little sister receives a friendly hug and a smile from her Big Sister on Stein Rediscovery.

A Big Sister finds some quiet time for a stroll in the dunes with a little brother on Rediscovery Four Corners.

many realize that some of the scariest stories are their own true-life experiences? Story Stick is designed to help expose these hidden fears and traumas, and help an individual get rid of a particular nightmare. This activity works best on the third or fourth night of camp, when the group members feel more comfortable with one another and open to deeper sharing. The staff can contribute some good scary stories at the previous night's campfire as a lead-in to this event, telling the group that each individual must bring a stick of wood as long as their arm to the next fire and that "... tomorrow night we are going to tell the scariest stories of all."

That night the fire is kept relatively small to gather the group in close. A group leader explains, "Every one of us has had a horrifying experience at some point during our lives, and tonight we are each going to have the opportunity to share that experience with our friends here." He or she begins, placing a stick on the fire, and as the flames consume the stick, the story unfolds. Once the leader finishes, the person to his or her left begins their story by first placing their stick on the fire. If an individual is not quite ready to share their story, continue on to the next person rather than try to force a response. Every one will contribute something when they are ready. Keep the flow moving clockwise at all times.

Very often the stories will start out rather light — ghost stories, or some wild animal scare. Eventually they may shift to accidents and tragic losses of loved ones. The more deeply one individual shares, the deeper the share response is triggered in the group. Attempted suicide, child battering, molesting, and rape may be openly acknowledged and shared for the first time. Some individuals will need the comforting support of those around them.

Let them know they are not alone. Remind them that much of that nightmare now lies behind them. Point out that no one in the group is without pain, fear, or emotional scars. Privately, let those most distressed or the victims of crime know that help is available to them through a social worker, mental-health worker, or the police. Story Stick can be a powerful emotional experience. Do not treat this activity lightly or engage in it unless the staff are confident they can cope with the situation. Also be fully aware of the legal responsibility to report disclosures of crimes committed against a child to a social worker or police officer.

Allow a full evening for Story Stick, as it can run very late, especially if the group is large.

Centre Circle

A possible follow-up to youth who exposed deep scars during Story Stick, or to anyone feeling in the slightest way unappreciated or dejected, is to put them in Centre Circle. The group forms a large circle, holding hands and facing inward. Everyone's attention and admiration focuses on a person standing in the middle, there solely to be complimented. "Okay, now we're all going to say something we honestly like about Susan," the instructor begins. (Sincerity of comment is critical to the success of this exercise.) "I didn't know you at first, Susan," the instructor says, "but I really think you'd be a good friend to have." The next person in the circle addresses Susan: "I saw you share your candy yesterday with someone who didn't have any. I think you're a caring person." The next: "I like the way you wear your hair, Susan. It's cute." And so on down the line. Susan is being inflated like a balloon by admiration. Disbelievers should try standing in the middle of a Centre Circle. Following a Centre Circle experience at a community workshop in Powell River, an officer of the Royal Canadian Mounted Police commented, "Boy, do I feel good. I didn't think anyone here appreciated me."

LOOKING INWARD

How many of us reflect on the food we've been blessed with before a meal, sit in solitude and absorb the beauty of nature with all our being, take time at sunset to think back on the day behind and the days yet ahead, or spend a full day and night isolated from all others, looking inward at the person we are or want to become? Native North Americans, indeed, spiritual people throughout the world, have always known that deep insight and self-awareness comes most powerfully through solitude. It is easy to get caught up in the activities and group energy of a camp experience and never really tune in to the intimacies of the wilderness itself. Rediscovery schedules time for quiet introspection, with looking-inward opportunities every day.

Readings

Reading an appropriate passage from a favourite book, a poem, scripture, or quote, provides a quiet reflective moment before meals. Initially the staff will have to conduct this exercise, but once the spirit of the event catches on, the participants will begin to contribute their own original material. A wonderful way to settle everyone down a bit before meals, Readings also make a nice lead-in to a more formal prayer if an elder or someone in the group would like to offer a blessing. Reflecting on the day's activities, the days behind, and those yet to come, and giving thanks for the rich bounty of food everyone will soon share adds a spiritual dimension to an activity we all too often take for granted. It also instills a sense of family, and reminds all of their place in the natural world.

Examples:

"Now I see the secret of making the best persons — it is to grow in the open air and to eat and sleep with the earth."

— Walt Whitman

"Go to the mountains and get their good tidings — Nature's peace will flow into you as sunshine flows into trees, The winds will blow their freshness into you, And the storms their energy, While cares will drop off like autumn leaves."

— John Muir

"Stealing from mice is something I never did but aunt and grandmother told me about it. They would go off in the brush, in the woods, and steal wild beans from the mice. These mice know how to store things. Running back and forth, the mice carried things to a particular place. Their little trails showed the way they went into their holes in the ground. There they gathered very many of those wild beans. Grandmother said that when a family had a lot of little boys, it used to be said of the last born, the youngest one, that he is married to one of these mice. It was that boy who used to find the storehouses ... the beans that we eat today are good, but wild beans are much more delicious."

— Mountain Wolf Woman, from *The Autobiography of a Winnebago Indian*

"I do not think that the measure of a civilization is how tall its buildings of concrete are, but rather how well its people have learned to live with their environment and fellow man."

— Sun Bear (Chippewa)

"Sometimes I share my bread and jam with yellowjackets, who have a home on the bush by the road, twenty trees and one distant from the garden. Today I climbed upon the old rail fence close to their home, with a piece and a half of bread and jam — and the half piece for them, and the piece for myself. But they all wanted to be served at once, so it

Spirit Spot provides time for quiet introspection and intimate nature observation every day.

became necessary to turn over all bread and jam on hand. I broke it into little pieces, and they had a royal feast there on the old fence-rail. I wanted my bread and jam — but then yellowjackets are such interesting fairies, being among the world's first paper-makers; and baby yellowjackets are such chubby youngsters. Thinking of these things makes it a joy to share one's bread and jam with these wasp fairies."

— Opal Whiteley (six years old), from *The Singing Creek Where the Willows Grow: The Rediscovered Diary of Opal Whiteley*

Spirit Spot

People with Western secular biases find it difficult to imagine a place imbued with power — much less suited to a specific individual. North American indigenous peoples recognized the special powers which could come to a person by placing oneself in the right frame of mind and the right location. Spirit Spot tries to reintroduce youth to this experience, as well as provide a scheduled time for quiet introspection and intimate nature observation every day.

For this exercise to be successful, the staff must prepare youngsters psychologically. Just sending them off alone each day can be too much like a "Go stand in the corner" punishment. Tell the participants of the native traditions where youth their age would spend long periods alone in search of spirit guardians, the opportunity they will have every day to see the same place under different conditions — sunny, shady, windy, calm, wet, and foggy — and the many animals that might approach them if they're quiet: birds, chipmunks, squirrels, and deer. Above all, tell them that this exercise will help them prepare for their Solo/Vision Quest later in the program, when they will have an opportunity to spend twenty-four hours completely alone.

In finding Spirit Spots a few rules must be observed: first, no individual should be in view of another, or in view of the camp proper. Second, silence must be maintained at all times, so the experience is not ruined for others. Third, once a Spirit Spot has been chosen (in a forest, along a stream, or on the shoreline), the youngster is duty-bound to return to that same spot each day. The leader must explain the signal for the end of the Spirit Spot — a conch-shell blast or loud drumbeat. Schedule this exercise early in the day, after camp chores, or in the evenings near sunset. Reserve the same time period every day for this thirty- to forty-five-minute exercise. Don't make Spirit Spot too short (or it will be meaningless), or too long (as some youngsters will complain of boredom). It may be necessary for the staff to monitor campers at their Spirit Spots for the first few days or until a routine is established.

On the third or fourth day of the exercises, give all participants paper and watercolours, crayons, felt pens, or coloured pencils. Ask them to try putting the images from their Spirit Spot on paper. It needn't be a photographic image, perhaps just colours. Tell the campers to fully express themselves, as these paintings are confidential. On the following day, give everyone a pen and paper and ask them to write a letter to themselves — "Dear Me." Ask them to express how they feel about their lives up to that point, how they feel then and there at their Spirit Spot, and what they imagine themselves to be like three years into the future. The letters, strictly confidential, should close with a loving salutation and signature. Both the paintings and the letters should be sealed in an envelope addressed to the youngster they belong to, and mailed out to them three years after they leave the program.

Nature's Orchestra and Shared Vision, described later, are other activities ideally suited to Spirit Spot time.

Viewing Party

Viewing Party is a delightful event for that occasional camp participant feeling a little homesick, lonely, or troubled in some personal way. A staff member creates a simple but very personal invitation card, hand-painted or decorated with pressed flowers, feathers, or leaves. Then they secretly slip the card to the troubled youngster sometime during the day. It reads: "You are cordially invited to a private Viewing Party this evening. Meet me behind the cookhouse thirty minutes before sunset. Tell no one!" At the arranged time, the staff member meets the youngster and leads him or her off to any beautiful and private setting — sea cliff, a meadow, stream bank, or hilltop where the sunset can be viewed. To the youngster's surprise the staff member pulls a tea set out of a pack, sets out a tablecloth, pours tea, and serves homemade cookies, tarts, or cakes.

The staff member explains that it's very important at a Viewing Party to not talk until after the sun drops below the horizon. "Let's just sip our tea quietly together and reflect on how special we and this evening are." Silence comes easily. Even wars have been known to observe cease-fire during sunset. Sunset is, for most people, the most reflective moment of the day.

The moment the sun disappears, the staff member may break the silence by sharing some thoughts of his or her own and encouraging the youngster to do the same. A wonderful closing to the Viewing Party is

A Viewing Party at sunset can be a special experience for a camp participant feeling homesick, or troubled in some personal way.

to read the tea leaves in the youngster's empty cup. "Ahh, yes, I can see that you have had some worries lately. Notice that clump of leaves at the bottom of the cup — very confused. But there's a leaf heading away from the bottom, looks like bright times ahead."

Self-Esteem Backpack

Self-Esteem Backpack, a creative visualization exercise, helps empower youngsters to be all that they can be. Through the power of suggestion and cultural imagery, players emerge from this exercise with a renewed sense of self-worth and self-confidence.

A virgin-forest setting with relaxing natural sounds and a deep bed of moss, needles, or soft leaves to lie on would be the quintessential environment for Self-Esteem Backpack. It can be done, however, in any peaceful setting — even indoors with relaxing background music. Creative visualization works well at night, just before sleeping, because the mind and body are often already deeply relaxed and receptive. An evening during an overnight hike or expedition presents an ideal opportunity for Self-Esteem Backpack.

Have the participants lie on their backs, close their eyes, and breathing slowly and deeply, relaxing each muscle in their body one at a time while the instructor counts very slowly from ten to one. As in all creative visualization, the instructor's voice, mood, and power of suggestion will be the key to success in this exercise.

Haida Gwaii's Rediscovery uses the following example, focussing on the rainforest and Haida culture. The story should be appropriate to both the indigenous culture and the area the exercise occurs in.

"Imagine yourself walking through a great forest of ancient trees," the instructor begins, after everyone has relaxed. "Moss hangs from every branch and carpets the forest floor in a million shades of green. From somewhere high in the forest canopy, a thrush sings a long note. Huge roots clutch the ground, each one a fantastic figure. Everything about this place seems enchanted and you feel very much at peace. Up ahead the sun streams through an opening in the forest canopy, sending shafts of light down through the cool, moisture-laden air. The light illuminates something red and alluring. You find yourself magically drawn to it. There, at the base of a huge cedar tree, rests a beautiful red backpack. You are amazed to see it has your name on it. When you look inside you see great treasures.

"There is a gift from Raven, a beautiful dance-mask headdress to remind you of your curiosity and desire to learn. You put the headdress on and suddenly you want to explore all things, to discover new people and places, to learn more in every way about the world. Like the raven, your curiosity will never be fully satisfied. Wear your raven headdress like a graduation cap and gown, even when others try to tell you that you will not succeed.

"Now you look again into your backpack, and find a gift from Eagle, a wing feather to give you the courage to express yourself. When you hold the eagle feather you have no trouble speaking — even in front of strangers. The feather reminds you that, like the eagle, you too are free, free to share with others your feelings, your fears, your hopes, and, yes, even your hurts. Remember to always speak from the heart and speak the truth when you hold your feather.

"There is another gift in your backpack — a painted bent-cedar box. The design on the box displays your crest (or coat of arms), so you know this treasure is for you. Inside the box are two stones from Sea Otter to remind you of your many skills and resources. Like the tool-using sea otter, who uses stones to crack open urchins, mussels, and clams, you too have many skills to help you in life. Remember to always be expanding your skills, to fill your cedar box with more tools for life all the time.

"There is something more in the backpack — a carved wooden bear pole. The little totem pole is a gift from Grizzly Bear. It is to remind you of your strength and courage. There will be times in life when you will need to draw on these powers to protect yourself and to do extraordinary tasks. Remember that the strength and power comes from within and that even superior physical strength must be used appropriately — like a mother bear defending her young or overturning a log for her cubs to eat insects. Use your bear pole wisely.

"You reach down into the bottom of your backpack and find one final gift, so small that it was easy to overlook until now, a shining copper medallion. It is a gift from the earth to remind you to express your choices. One side of the medallion has your face on it, the other side is blank. The two sides represent your ability to say yes and no. Always wear your medallion proudly, for you are a totally unique and special person. Show appreciation for yourself by wearing your face side of the medallion visible for all to see. There will be times when your sense of self-worth will be challenged and people will not appreciate you for who you are, or will try to make you do things against your will. Remember your ability to say no at such times, and turn your medallion around. 'That's not me,' you will tell yourself. Remember, if you stay true

Self-Esteem Backpack uses cultural imagery to build self-confidence in participants.

Outfitted with only two matches, a raw potato, and a sleeping bag,
a young Haida girl is dropped off at her Solo/Vision Quest site.

A Haida boy builds a shelter of driftwood to keep him dry during his Solo/Vision Quest.

to yourself, you will never be false to another."

The instructor now has the participants return all their gifts to their backpack one at a time, reminding them again what each represents. "Now take a deep breath before you shoulder your pack, for you'll be going on a long, long journey," the instructor concludes. "Wow! The pack is surprisingly light and very comfortable. That's good. It will be easy to carry on your journey through life."

The Solo / Vision Quest

Vision questing has been the traditional rite of passage on the North American continent for thousands of years. Indians marked the transition from childhood to adulthood with long periods of isolation, fasting, and meditation in the wilderness in search of spirit guardians. Some native peoples still pursue vision quests as the highest form of Native American religion, held so sacred that it borders on heresy to mention the practice in this context. Mention is made merely to distinguish between the solo experience of many adventure programs and the more culturally attuned and spiritual focus of Solo/Vision Quests. Through the careful guidance of native elders and spiritual leaders, Rediscovery participants can take part in a time-honoured rite of passage. The benefits of this traditional approach for youth in the twentieth century are so profound that the Solo/Vision Quest has become Rediscovery's greatest key for unlocking the doors to self-discovery.

Smoking a cigarette, graduating from high school, getting a driver's licence, voting, being old enough to drink in bars or go to jail: these events mark the transition from childhood to adulthood in our Western society. Usually void of spirituality, they range over a number of years without any one event whereby a child becomes accepted as an adult. By contrast, tribal societies clearly distinguish this important stage in personal development. Chief Tetlaneetsa of Spences Bridge recalls his rite of passage in 1912:

"Now I understand the words of my old grandfather:

'When you wake in the mountains at daybreak, you shall hear the voice of Nature. Listen to it, my son, for it holds great treasures for you!'

"I listened to the voice of the wind, the voice from the valley below growing louder with the light of dawn!

"Its song brushed the grass, the fireweeds, the bushes.

"It swept the treetops, the trees large and small, the trees with leaves and the evergreens with needles.

"It was the song of the morning wind that makes Nature sing — The rivers, the canyons, the mountain gorges, the forests, the wild fruit patches at timberline, and the peaks glittering with snow.

"They were all singing in the wind. Under their breath as they still sang, I passed from childhood to the rising power of a man."

At the age of fourteen, Frank Brown, founder of Heiltsuk Rediscovery, was left alone in the wilderness for almost a year. Here, he tells of his personal rites of passage:

Rebirth of the Winalha Spirit

Defender of the people
In ages past with bow and arrow
In contemporary time with pen and paper

In defense of our Native homelands
And their embodied resources
I am of the Winalha Spirit
A warrior in training.

I have gone through a rite of passage

I have learned the ways of the Enemy
I have defied the odds and met success —
VICTORY

The spirit of Winalha, the warrior
And protector of the people
Must be passed on to new generations
Of our native youth
For the continuation of our race.
May God guide us in our struggle.

Rediscovery Solos resemble those of some other programs in the sense that an individual stays alone in the wilderness for a twenty-four-hour period with little food and other resources: water, two or three matches, a pen and paper for recording thoughts, a sleeping bag, and a cooking pot. But Rediscovery Solos differ from most camp solos in some important many ways. First, no participant is required to take part in this event and no participant will be put down for not doing so. The achievement is far greater when one approaches it of their own free will. Second, ceremonies marking the beginning and end of the Solo experience are in keeping with the traditions of the indigenous local culture and are, whenever possible, presided over by native elders. These might include food offerings on a fire to the ancestors who have gone before, smudging (smoke purifications with sweet grass, sage, or cedar), pipe ceremonies (tobacco offerings to the sacred directions), and ceremonial sweat lodges for purification. Third, the entire camp connects in spirit with those on their Solos. The group lights a vigil fire during the ceremony just prior to the soloists' departure. Those remaining in camp take turns keeping a silent vigil by this fire throughout the twenty-four-hour period. The vigil fire not only acts as a quiet reflective place for those not on Solo, but also provides an important transition zone for those returning to camp either early (through unsuccessful attempts to stay out) or at the completion of their quest.

It is extremely important to prepare participants psychologically for the Solo/Vision Quest. Native elders can be particularly effective in this regard, describing how children once did this when there were far more wild and dangerous animals than today. The late Wilfred Bennett, a Haida elder, told a group of soloists, "If you can learn to live in harmony with this experience, it will carry over into the rest of your life."

Drawing on all his skills and resources, a Rediscovery soloist succeeds in lighting a fire with one of his two matches.

Native elders and staff at Rediscovery Four Corners keep vigil throughout the night, ready to counsel any soloist returning early to base camp.

Ironically, a decade of Rediscovery programs shows that the younger the person, the more likely they are to volunteer for Solo and the more likely to successfully complete it. Pre-teens average success rates of about eighty-five percent, teens about sixty-five to seventy percent and adults less than fifty percent. What this suggests about confidence building as one grows older is the exact opposite of what one would expect.

Another strange reversal occurs during Solos. A group bully or the top of the "pecking order" will almost always fail to complete this experience. A Haida elder once explained it this way: "The reason a child acts that way is because he doesn't know or like himself. Nobody wants to spend that much time alone with someone they don't know or like — especially if that person is yourself!"

Those "least likely to succeed" most often return successfully from Solos. Everyone wonders why the tough guys almost without exception fail in their Solo by coming back before dark. First impressions suddenly turn upside down in youngsters' minds. A necessary humbling experience for some, restoring self-pride for others. Solo does a lot more than develop self-confidence: it connects youngsters directly with the earth and themselves. "I thought the earth remembered me. She took me back so tenderly," wrote one young girl of her night curled up under a spruce tree. A boy wrote of his experience with fire charcoal on his driftwood shelter: "Here I am on solo night. At first it gave me quite a fright but when I see the swaying trees and hear the peaceful rhythm of the sea, I feel more confident in me."

Sometimes the lessons of a failed solo attempt can be as profound as the successful experience — or even amusing.

Carl MacIntyre returned to camp early from his solo, with an unusual story. He told of a bird that flew into his shelter, chirping "Come quickly! Come quickly!". Carl jumped up and followed the little wren down the beach, where it stood on a log, looked back at him, and chirped: "Too late! Too late!"

A word of caution. While the Solo/Vision Quest is a profound experience and highly recommended activity, care must be exercised to insure participant safety. Youngsters should never be located near natural hazards, i.e., avalanche slopes, grizzly-bear trails or well-known feeding locations, below high-tide lines, near creeks that flash flood, or below a tree that might be inclined to drop a large branch. Knives and hatchets, the number-one cause of injury in these situations, should be forbidden — especially with younger children. Fires should only be part of a Solo if all campers have been trained in proper fire building and safety and if forest-fire danger is extremely low or nil. Fires help a lot of youngsters through the experience, as a poem by a young girl, Dana Nyehold, out on her Solo, testifies:

Dancers

The firelight is dancing
and singing a beautiful song
black white orange and red
carry me through the dark hours I dread
The long wispy puffs of smoke
are whispering welcome to all
all alone with no company
except my firelight dancers

All fire locations should be carefully positioned by the staff. Finally, every participant's location should be recorded on a detailed map and a secret spot check should be made just prior to dark.

CHAPTER 2
CULTURAL WORLDS BETWEEN

The staff work all day to set up the four tipis for Rediscovery Four Corners in the high Colorado Valley, and the Ute Indian elders who oversee the project are satisfied. The tipis are aligned exactly north, east, south, and west: they each have their proper coloured prayer flags fluttering from the pole tops, and each tipi rests exactly equal distance from the others and the central fire pit. But now, as the sun sets on the eve before camp opens, the staff find a large red-ant mound inside the east tipi. Obviously children cannot bed down on top of fire ants, so the group must light the lanterns and prepare for a full night's work. The east tipi must be relocated: therefore, the other three tipis will have to be moved accordingly. The staff will have to work all night to have camp ready for the first arrivals in the morning. "Don't do anything more tonight," a Pueblo Indian elder and cultural director for the program says calmly, "I will talk to the ants in the morning." "Talk to the ants?" someone asks, unbelieving. "Yes, they are our ancestors. They helped us emerge from the underworld by providing us with food to grow big and strong while they stayed small. They have helped me find my way many times when I was lost." The Pueblo man speaks with such conviction that he almost overcomes some of the staff's scepticism. "Can you talk to them now?" someone asks impatiently. "No, they are still active and will bite,"

comes the sensible answer. "I will talk to them at dawn."

The predawn light has not yet penetrated the eastern tipi when the Pueblo elder places a pinch of cornmeal beside the ant hole and rests his head on the mound as if it were a pillow. "Dear ants," he whispers into the tiny hole, "I'm sorry to have woken you so early, but I've brought you some breakfast and come to ask of you a favour. We have made a mistake and put a tipi over top of your house. I ask this, not for me, but for the children who arrive today. Could you please move your house?" The staff erects a tarp under a piñon pine to temporarily house those participants not able to sleep in the east tipi. The tarp is never used. Hours later, the ants carry the last of their eggs out from under the tipi edge into a new hole four metres away. The children move in on schedule.

Rediscovery focuses on the sensitivity to and total immersion in different cultures. The renewed pride in cultural identity and skills that native youth experience on Rediscovery are easily matched by the sense of cross-cultural understanding experienced by non-natives. Rediscovery camps deal with multicultural mixes of people from widely divergent backgrounds. A Rediscovery Four Corners camp in Colorado may open with a Ute pipe ceremony, a Pueblo cornmeal blessing, a Christian prayer, and a Buddhist chant. Currently, natives from twenty-one North American tribal groups take part in Rediscovery programs: other participants and staff come from such diverse locations as Peru, Hawaii, Japan, Hong Kong, Bhutan, Germany, and Sweden.

Australians have expressed interest in modelling a program along the line of Rediscovery to help bridge the enormous gap between Anglo-Australian and Aborigine cultures. There have been similar suggestions for the Japanese and original Ainu inhabitants: the Carib Indians and the Anglo/Afro population of the Caribbean; Israelis and Palestinians; Chinese and Malays. Possibilities are endless, as the need for cultural tolerance and understanding has perhaps never been more critical in human history.

The following activities are designed to help remove some of our cultural blinders, to see that the human bond we share is far greater than our differences, to better understand some of the injustices cultures sometimes inflict on one another, so that history need not be repeated.

EXPLORING ROOTS

Western books, movies, and television have so largely ignored or distorted Indian history, culture, and traditions that today's native youth are sometimes as misinformed as their non-native classmates. The following activities are designed to give youngsters a deeper understanding of North American native nations and their firmly established roots. Different activities explore the roots of prejudice, misunderstanding, historic injustice, and stereotypes — many of which are still perpetuated today. How many people know that potatoes, corn, pumpkin squash, sunflower seeds, turkey, chocolate, and maple syrup were all foods eaten by Indians before Europeans ever heard of them? Or that historically, Indians have engaged in more battles alongside white men than against them? Or that the first white people on the American continent would not have survived without the Indians' generosity and help?

Through these activities cultural values are examined: What was life like in pre-contact North America? What happens when people of different cultural values interact? What happens to a culture whose values are in a state of rapid transition? Through humour, role-play, and group discussion, it is hoped that these activities will help native and non-native youth know more about where they've come from so they can have a better perspective on where they want to be going.

A certain skill level may be required by both staff and participants in order to fully actualize the potential of these role-play games. First and foremost is the need for a skilled animator/facilitator. Some of the activities are quite theatrically oriented. This is mentioned not to dissuade the intended animator, but rather to inform that theatrical or didactical games are quite an undertaking. Here are a few reminders and suggestions on group workings.

As far as participants go, trust games are a good way to "warm" them up to playing. (Some trust games are mentioned in the Bonding section.) Of course, after the trust games, it's up to the animator to decide if the dynamics of the group will allow for role-play and/or how best to proceed.

Safety is the key to effective play here. If the animator can set a "safe" atmosphere whereby everyone's right to play unashamedly is enforced, then all the games will unroll as intended. This is especially important for Role Reversal, for example, if you are to receive honest answers. Confrontation can happen without being destructive. Confidence and trust will flourish.

Also, let the participants take possession of the games. Again, it is up to the animator to decide if and when to intervene. The direction given by the animator must be gentle enough to steer the proceedings without stopping the inevitable and valuable tangents that can occur in the course of exploration in play or discussion.

The participants are just as responsible as the animator in terms of how the action is proceeding. Tell them this. Some may choose not to take part. It is then the animator's decision how best to engage him or her, if at all. It is sometimes best to allow the participants to take in the scene before they will venture into play.

Role-playing is a "safe" way to act out scenes from life. However, some painful feelings or memories may be triggered by the role-plays. It is important, then, that participants "cool down" by discussing what has gone on for each of them in the course of the games. It is quite healthy for them, in a group context, to learn to trust, nurture, and care for each other.

These activities should be modified to suit each group and individual culture. Age, setting, and level of trust between participants are other important considerations. These examples are offered as only a small contribution to what will hopefully become a unique collection of culturally appropriate role-play games for each Rediscovery Program.

A Day In The Life Of The Village

A Day in the Life of the Village helps youngsters gain some insight into the lives of native peoples prior to European contact. Traditional costumes and regalia (or even a trunkful of cloth, beads, and make-up) adds to the fun, and removes many inhibitions about acting. Set the scene in a culturally appropriate setting — an ancient village site, a cedar longhouse, tipi, pit house, or other cultural centre. Use traditional tools, baskets, or daily life items to lend greater authenticity to the role-play setting. Animal hides, furs, and feathers can often be acquired for such cultural use from Fish and Wildlife (Game) departments of government, which confiscate the remains of animals illegally taken.

Divide the participants into two village groups, with boys and girls and a few staff and elders in each group. Give each group a basket from which they will draw traditional role names, responsibilities, and secret motivation. For instance, in Haida Gwaii's Rediscovery, traditional Haida roles would be presented.

RAVEN VILLAGE

— You live in the Raven Village. You are a slave who was captured during battle and taken from your homeland eight years ago. You must obey all the members of the Head Chief's household.

Secret desire: To escape and return to your homeland.

— You are the Head Chief of the Raven Village and a feared warrior. You have taken many slaves, won many battles, and held many potlatches during your long life.

Secret desire: To have your nephew, the future chief, marry the princess of the Eagle Village to forge a bond of peace with your neighbouring village.

— You are the second nephew to the Head Chief and the best sea-lion hunter in the Raven Village. Many believe you should become the next chief, but the title properly goes to another.

Secret desire: To someday become a chief.

— You live in the Raven Village. You are the greatest warrior your village has ever known. You have made the Raven Chief's name great throughout the land.

Secret desire: Conquest of the Eagle Village.

— You are the wife of the great Raven Chief, but have never been given the recognition the Eagle Chief's wife enjoys.

Secret desire: To hold higher rank than the Eagle Chief's wife.

EAGLE VILLAGE

— You live in the Eagle Village. You are the Head Chief's oldest nephew and rightful heir to the chieftainship, though you are not as well liked as your uncle.

Secret desire: To hold more potlatches than your uncle.

— You live in the Eagle Village. You are a princess, the eldest daughter of the chief. You have a happy life picking berries, playing with your brothers and sisters, telling stories, helping your mother.

Secret desire: To run away with the slave of the Raven Chief and not marry the Raven Chief's nephew.

— You are the great Shaman of the Eagle Village. Your medicine is stronger than that of any other medicine man.

Secret desire: To pass on your powers to the Bear Chief before you die.

— You live in the Eagle Village. You are the Head Chief's wife. You are a woman of very high rank in the village, and have many slaves assisting you in your work.

Secret desire: To arrange the marriage of your daughter to the Raven Chief's nephew to secure more slaves.

— You are a sub-chief of the Eagle Village — the powerful Bear Chief, descendant of a mainland lineage.

Secret desire: To become a shaman.

— You are the great and powerful Eagle Chief. No other chief is higher in status except one — the Raven Chief of your neighbouring village.

A Day in the Life of the Village at Stein Rediscovery provides insight into the lives of native people prior to European contact.

Traditional Haida roles are acted out in A Day in the Life of the Village exercises on Haida Gwaii Rediscovery.

Secret desire: To amass enough wealth to hold a bigger potlatch than any held by the Raven Chief.

— You are an elder, the great-grandfather of the Eagle Chief and the oldest person in the village. Your wisdom is sought and respected by all your people.

Secret desire: To die knowing your people and the Raven Village will live in peace.

Male and female roles are divided into different baskets from which participants draw. Both villages will have similar sets of social roles.

Stories or historical accounts of the social life and traditions of the people told by the staff can help prepare the members of their group for the role-play prior to the actual exercise. Once the interaction between the two villages begins, however, the staff takes a back seat to the action. The intergroup dynamics can be fascinating to watch, with songs, dances, sorcery, and healings all part of the action. The way in which the villages interact depends totally on the youngsters. Arranged marriages binding the villages together in peace can be a result, or, on the other end of the spectrum, open hostilities with hostage- and property-taking. The elders advise their village group on correct behaviour if the role-play starts to veer too sharply away from tradition.

This activity can last from an hour-long story play to an epic involving the better part of the day. If participants have difficulty setting their own scene, the staff and elders can assist and enter the action with assigned roles of their own.

It is one thing to gain insight into precontact native cultures from books and quite another to act out a day in the life of a village more than a century ago. An interesting follow-up activity to this would be to update the role-play to Today in the Life of a Village. Participants might be surprised to see more continuity with the past than they might at first expect. Compare the similarities and the differences with the earlier role-play.

Early Contact

Fascinating historical accounts tell of the first contact between peoples of widely divergent cultures. At times these encounters were simply humorous, but more often they resulted in serious misunderstandings, with sometimes tragic consequences.

When Indians on the eastern American seaboard first encountered Europeans taking their Victorian lace handkerchiefs from their pocket to blow their nose, then carefully folding them back into a breast pocket near the heart, they naturally assumed that snot was something white men cherished. (The Indians simply cleared their sinuses by pressing against one nostril and snorting the other toward the ground.)

Other encounters were far more serious. Violation of social customs could wittingly or unwittingly produce conflict. A classic case occurred on Haida Gwaii in 1789, when a Boston trader, Captain John Kendrick, returned to trade for furs with the Haidas. Although the first visit by Kendrick resulted in amicable trade, a minor incident on the second visit triggered years of bloody conflict.

Pilfering minor items from a ship's deck was common practice by Indians boarding trading vessels at that time, and most captains over-looked these minor losses so as not to impede the lucrative trade in furs. Kendrick, however, awakening drunk to see that some of his personal laundry had disappeared from a clothesline, reacted irrationally. The Haida chief Koyah was taken hostage at gunpoint and publicly humiliated before his people. A rope was tied around his neck, his hair cut off, his face painted, and he was whipped until all the furs in his village were brought to Kendrick's boat. To show that he was a "civilized" man, Kendrick paid a token fee for each of the furs before he released the chief and departed.

Koyah was no longer a chief now in his people's eyes, but one of lower class. The only way he could restore his rank was to seek revenge. A great loss of life ensued, involving many Haidas and some innocent trading vessels.

Early Contact helps participants realize that not all peoples share the same values, customs, and social mores. Any number of people can take part in this exercise as long as they are divided into two distinct groups, ideally with males and females present in each.

The object of the game is simply to engage in trading, but this can be tricky given no common language between the two groups and very different social values. A dozen kerchiefs and a dozen butter knives make good trade items. The group with the kerchiefs may choose to adorn themselves in them (headbands, wristbands, et cetera), to distin-guish themselves from the group with the knives. Assign each group a private-village or trade-ship location where they may speak freely amongst themselves without being overheard by the other group. Now give each group an index card with the name of their group and a set of cultural values they must abide by. The index cards for Group A and Group B might read as follows:

GROUP A — ALCANS

You are aggressive traders, very clever, always out to get the best possible deal. Men are usually dominant in trade negotiations.

Knives are a hot commodity — all the tribespeople in this region want them.

You show your straightforward willingness to trade using direct eye contact, a good firm handshake, and possibly a friendly pat on the back.

Each of you is out for yourself, trying to acquire as much cloth as possible because it brings a good price back home.

Get as much as you can from these people: after all, they are uneducated savages in your mind — their culture is certainly not as advanced as your own.

GROUP B — BUMBAS

Your society is Matriarchal — the eldest woman is the leader, and only she can engage in the direct act of trading. Others in your tribe can only bring traders to her.

The matriarch signals her willingness to trade by waving her hand back and forth between herself and the person she desires to trade with. (Demonstrate: like shooing away a dog.)

You do not look strangers directly in the eye and no one outside your tribe must ever touch you. To break this taboo results in banishment from your people. It is especially important that your matriarch not be contaminated by the touch of others.

You always do everything as a group — even trading — and no one works toward personal gain.

You could use some knives for cutting food, but you are reluctant to trade too much cloth, for it is handwoven by your matriarch and very sacred to your culture.

You are a peaceful people — slow to anger, but you do have great pride and expect to be treated with utmost respect.

These tribal names are fictitious but the sets of cultural values closely parallel some real world cultures. Once the Bumbas and Alcans have had a few minutes to review and discuss their values, they are given their respective trade items and signalled to come together for the first of three two- to three-minute trading sessions. (The designated trading area must be large enough to accommodate both groups as clearly distinct entities.) During trading, either group may use gestures and any sound, short of actual language, to attempt to communicate. At the end of each trade session, the Bumbas return to their village and the Alcans

Early contact between Indians and Europeans often led to trade, but sometimes resulted in serious misunderstandings.

to their trade vessel to discuss amongst themselves how to better facilitate the trading. Strategies may be devised, and a sensitive group might even begin to modify their customs to help facilitate the process.

The most important part of the exercise comes at the completion of the three trade periods, when both groups sit opposite one another and Group A describes what they think the values of Group B were. Then Group B does the same for Group A. (Some refereeing may be in order here, as the exchange can get heated.) More often than not, each group developed a dislike for the other and considered their counterparts stingy, ruthless, and somewhat barbaric. On rare occasions, a level of understanding may emerge, with some successful trading completed and both parties satisfied.

Once the two groups have stated what they thought the values of the other were, have a person in each group read out loud their actual values.

Reversing History

Caucasians often fail to fully comprehend the impact their culture has had on indigenous North Americans. One frequently hears the callous comments: "We must do something about the Indian problem," or "It's too bad they've given up so much of their culture." Such statements reflect an enormous ignorance of the injustice that continues, in many areas, to this day. Reversing History, a light-hearted theatrical presentation, uses humour to convey the impact one culture on this continent has had on another. The script can be greatly elaborated upon. It can be presented simply as a fireside story, but is much more effective and fun if the camp staff (both native and non-native) act it out. Some of the program participants can also play roles as long as they have a flair for theatrics and some knowledge of the historical situation they are trying to portray in reverse.

A staff narrator begins the play by setting the stage: "Not long ago there was a happy, healthy, prosperous people who lived rich and colourful lives in their suburban home communities. Every family had two or three cars in the garage, computer terminals in their home offices, and a television in every bedroom. They ate out often at fast-food outlets, sent their children to the best of schools, and spent their holidays in exotic sun destinations all over the world.

"All this changed with the coming of the Red Men. The Red Men arrived from a distant continent by canoe. It had been a long journey, and they were more than a little bit lost. Because they thought they had reached Turkey, they named the suburban people they discovered Turkeys. The Red Men were welcomed by the Turkeys and acted friendly at first. They even traded a few beaver skins for computers. But, deep down, the Red Men knew that the Turkeys were savages and would have to be civilized, like themselves.

"They began to remove the Turkeys from their suburban home environments, taking them deep into the wilderness to become like Red Men. The Turkeys were made to wear loincloths and long braided hair, and their children were punished whenever they spoke Turkey talk. They would have to learn Red Men language if they were ever to become civilized. Sometimes there were Turkey uprisings that had to be put down with the Red Men's superior arrow power.

"The Red Men searched all over the continent for Turkeys still practising their heathen religions. They forced the Turkeys to burn down their churches, throw away their Bibles, and go on spirit quests deep in the forest without food or water. Eventually the Turkeys realized that this was the way their world would be from now on. Many were depressed. They wanted to eat fast food hamburgers, not dried moose meat and whale blubber. Some Turkeys took to drinking too much of the Red Men's firewater to try to drown their sorrow.

"The Red Men were sensitive to the Turkey's lost way of life. They even set up museums to view the old computers, video games, acid-washed jeans, and hamburger wrappings of these noble savages. Some of the Turkeys were encouraged to do disco dancing for the amusement of Red Men tourists. Still, none of this seemed to help. The Turkeys were becoming a real burden to the Red Men. Even the Department of Turkey Affairs couldn't seem to find the solution. It was costing the Red Men a lot of whale muktuk and moose meat keeping all those Turkeys on welfare. Yes, something would have to be done about the Turkey problem: 'It's too bad the Turkeys have given up so much of their culture.' "

Some discussion should necessarily follow this exercise to help everyone better understand the parallels of this story with actual history. The instructor may want to discuss some of the historical impact on native cultures: treaties, military campaigns, introduced diseases, relocation, trade, alcohol, residential schools, reserve and reservation systems, Indian agencies, and potlatch laws. Some historical narratives can be read aloud to further discussion and understanding. Example:

"In 1774, the chiefs of the Six Nations protested strongly to Benjamin Franklin about the imposition of European education on Indian youth.

One of them observed: 'But you, who are wise, must know that different nations have different conceptions of things; and you will therefore not take it amiss, if our ideas of this kind of education happen not to be the same with yours. We have had some experience of it — several of our young people were formerly brought up at the colleges of the northern provinces; they were instructed in all your sciences, but when they came back to us, they were bad runners, ignorant of every means of living in the woods, unable to bear either cold or hunger, knew neither how to build a cabin, take a deer, or kill an enemy, spoke our language imperfectly, were therefore neither fit for hunters, warriors, nor coun-sellors; they were totally good for nothing. We are however not the less obliged by your kind offer, though we decline accepting it, and, to show our grateful sense of it, if the gentlemen of Virginia will send us a dozen of their sons, we will take great care of their education, instruct them in all we know, and make men of them.' "

Maquinna, 'Professor of pebbles,' was a Nootka chief who in 1896 defended the potlatch, which had been prohibited by an amendment to the Indian Act in 1884.

"I have always been kind to the white men.... And now I hear that the white chiefs want to persecute us and put us in jail and we do not know why.

"They say it is because we give feasts which the Chinook people call Potlatch. That is not bad! That which we give away is our own! Dr. Powell, the Indian agent, one day also made a potlatch to all the Indian chiefs, and gave them a coat, and tobacco, and other things, and thereby we all knew that he was a chief; and so when I give a potlatch, they all learn that I am a chief. To put in prison people who steal and sell whiskey and cards to our young men; that is right. But do not put us in jail as long as we have not stolen the things which we give away to our Indian friends. Once I was in Victoria, and I saw a very large house; they told me it was a bank and that the white men place their money there to take care of, and that by-and-by they got it back, with interest. We are Indians, and we have no such bank; but when we have plenty of money or blankets, we give them away to other chiefs and people, and by-and-by they return them, with interest, and our heart feels good. Our potlatch is our bank.

"I have given many times a potlatch, and I have more than two thousand dollars in the hands of Indian friends. They all will return it some time, and I will thus have the means to live when I cannot work any more. My uncle is blind and cannot work, and that is the way he now

"At first I didn't want to go on Rediscovery," said the boy buried for fun up to his neck; "being white in an Indian camp, I figured I'd be picked on."

lives, and he buys food for his family when the Indians make a potlatch. I feel alarmed! I must give up the potlatch or else be put in jail. Is the Indian agent going to take care of me when I can no longer work? No, I know he will not. He does not support the old and poor now. He gets plenty of money to support his own family, but although it is all our money, he gives nothing to our old people, and so it will be with me when I get old and infirm...

"Maquinna, X (his mark) Chief of Nootka."

The object of this exercise is not to lay any burden of guilt on the non-native participants, but for all to realize the enormity and absurdity of what actually took place, and in many ways is still taking place.

Role Reversal

Many native and non-native youth come to Rediscovery with preconceived notions or racist attitudes. When native and non-native youth display racist feelings, they are deliberately put in even closer association with one another. Since prejudice is largely based on ignorance, these forced encounters not only dispel many fallacies but also result in some new lifelong friendships.

Similarly, Role Reversal confronts racial attitudes head on. Each participant is asked in turn to contribute to a list of all the things they dislike about the other race. There are two lists growing on flip charts — native dislikes about whites and white dislikes of natives.

Examples:

I hate the way white people try to act superior by using big fancy words all the time.

Indians act so tough all the time. I feel like they try to bully me.

I don't like to drink, and I hate it when one of my Indian friends says, "What's the matter with you? Are you too white to drink with us?"

White people always try to act so good; they talk like drinking is just an Indian problem.

The list grows, the wounds are opening; time for staff guidance: "Okay, we're going to act out some of these situations, only you're going to reverse roles and become that person that you don't like." Native and non-native staff members begin acting out two of the listed grievances (or some added dislikes of their own). The participants are now encouraged to do the same. They may role-play individually, in pairs, or in a group, trying to portray as accurately as possible the other group's disliked behaviour or attitudes. For the first time in their lives, many will see themselves, and their behaviour, as they are perceived by others.

It is now time to heal the wounds. "I wonder if we could try composing two more lists?" a staff member offers. "This time let's list those things we actually like or admire in the other race. Any suggestions?" "I like the Indians' sense of extended family," a white girl acknowledges, "I think there's somehow more caring there than in our society." "White people are pretty smart with some of their inventions," a native child says. "Yeah, I like their music," another native boy adds. A non-native participant adds, "Indians are really generous, they always seem to be sharing everything." "They seem closer to nature in many ways, too," another white child contributes.

Let the likes list grow and grow — there will always be more of these than the dislikes. A remarkable bond can form in the group following this initial confrontation. Encourage this new feeling of closeness and understanding by concluding Role Reversal with a Circle Hug or a Centre Circle exercise with the two groups taking a turn in the complimentary centre.

Role Reversal can be applied to many forms of prejudice but is only used on Rediscovery following expressed prejudices. There are many hidden prejudices between differing races, cultures, religions, and nations. This activity can just as easily take place between Americans and Canadians, Christians and Muslims, or Blacks and Chicanos. Try some one-on-one discussions between individuals following the initial exercise.

Frontier/Homeland

"As an inferior race ... we believe [the Indian] must give way in order to make room for a race more enlightened, and by nature and habits better fitted to perform the task of converting what is now wilderness into productive fields and happy homes."
— British colonist, 1861

"We did not think of the great open plains, the beautiful rolling hills, and winding streams with tangled growth as 'wild'. Only to the white man was nature a 'wilderness' and only to him was the land 'infested' with 'wild' animals and 'savage' people. To us it was tame. Earth was bountiful and we were surrounded with the blessing of the Great Mystery. Not until the hairy man from the east came and with brutal frenzy heaped injustices upon us and the families we loved was it 'wild' for us. When the very animals of the forest began fleeing from his approach, then it was that for us the 'wild west' began."
— Chief Luther Standing Bear (Ogala Sioux)

Nowhere is the division more pronounced between North America's first peoples and the newcomers than in their different perceptions of wilderness as homeland or frontier. We see the dichotomy in thinking throughout our shared histories and, sadly, much in evidence today. Contemporary confrontations over land development or resource extraction (oil, natural gas, coal, timber, minerals, fish, wildlife, water) almost without exception involve native groups trying to protect their homeland from industries promising progress, jobs, and government revenues by developing these last frontiers.

Frontier/Homeland uses role-play exercise to explore these two world views. Cut five large index cards in two — each card should be cut in different shapes. Now print a position statement on half of each card so that opposing positions match up when the two pieces fit together.

Having requested the tree's permission, a Haida elder carefully strips bark from a cedar tree for weaving hats and baskets.

"The cedar tree is the cornerpost of our culture; our people have always used the forest without destroying it."

Examples:

Bison are the mainstay
of our Plains Indians life.
They provide us with food, hides,
tipis, clothing, and bedding.
They are sacred animals:
without them our
way of life would
vanish.

Open-range bison wreck
our fences and trample
our crops. We cannot
parcel out the west into
homesteads until bison
are eliminated. They
and the Indians
are in the way
of progress.

Caribou are our lifeblood. They return to our land
every summer to feed and clothe us. Oil
pipelines will disrupt their
ancient migrations
and our way
of life.

A lot more
people need oil in
the southern cities than
Indians and Inuit need caribou
in the North. The natives can get
jobs on the pipeline and
buy food like the rest of us.

The cedar tree is the cornerpost
of our culture. It provides
us with materials for
houses, canoes, totem
poles, boxes, bowls, hats,
and even clothing. Our people
have always used the
forest without destroying it.

The forests in the Pacific Northwest are over-mature and
decadent. We need to clear-cut
them quickly to grow more trees
for the pulp and lumber mills
which provide jobs, and build
homes and boost our economy.
Logging employs Indians too.

Our trails and traplines
on this land go back to
the beginning of time.
This is our home.
The Creator put
us here after the first
flood to care for this land.
Why don't the white men go
back where they came from?

The proposed dam will only
flood a vast wasteland of
stunted trees, bug-filled
swamps, and rodents. The few
Indians can move elsewhere.
We'll compensate them.
The city needs
that hydro power.

106

Our ancient prophesies tell us that we cannot tear the skin from our mother, the earth. If we remove minerals from deep under the ground it will mark the end of time. Black Mesa is sacred.

There's an energy crisis in our country and we cannot rely on foreign sources. We must develop the coal- and uranium-rich regions of the Southwestern States. Indian prophesies must not stand in the way of national interest.

Distribute pieces of the puzzles to each participant and ask them to find their opposing-viewpoint partner. After everyone matches up, the pairs find a private space to engage in one-on-one discussions. Each partner must hold the conviction of their position as they try to work out a solution between their opposing world views. The instructor should circulate between the parties to further challenge their thinking or answer any questions.

After fifteen to twenty minutes of discussion, call the participants together in front of a flip chart or blackboard scoreboard labelled: Frontier/Homeland. Have each team state their position to the group and explain any agreement they may have reached. Following each presentation, the instructor should describe what has been the actual outcome in each of the historic confrontations the students were presented with. Examples:

	Frontier	Homeland
The Plains bison	1	0
The Alaska pipeline	1	0
North Pacific Coast logging	1	0
The James Bay dam	1	0
Black Mesa coal mine	1	0

Each example should be briefly commented upon. "Why is the concept of homeland always on the losing end of these issues?" Discuss some exceptions to the rule, such as the Haida's successful defence of part of their homeland from logging. "Can we continue treating our continent as frontier," the instructor asks, "or do we need to start behaving as though we intend to stay?" "What does homeland mean to each of you?"

On the blackboard or flip chart, make a column for each participant's name and another for family background. "Where were you born?" the instructor asks each youngster, while filling in the place beside each

Connecting with an ancient past, a Thompson Indian boy fleshes a marmot skin on Stein Rediscovery.

name. "Where were your parents born?" Everyone then records where their grandparents were born, and then, if possible, their great-grandparents. Anyone that can trace their ancestry back further should be encouraged to do so. Next, ask each participant what language they suppose their distant relatives spoke: what kind of food they ate; what type of house they lived in. Then count how many of the group had ancestors from North America, South America, Europe, Asia, Africa, the Middle East .... "Where is your homeland?" the instructor finally asks. "How long do you have to be part of a place to belong?" Consider the sense of belonging to a place a very, very long time — ten to fifty thousand years. Discuss the words of Chief Luther Standing Bear: "In the Indian, the spirit of the land is still vested; it will be until other men are able to divine and meet its rhythm. Men must be born and reborn to belong. Their bodies must be formed of the dust of their forefather's bones."

Finally, have the group consider the concept of homeland as an attitude rather than a particular place. "What would the world be like if we all started thinking and behaving like this were our homeland and not a stepping stone to the stars?"

SHARING TRADITIONS

Sharing is a value central to most native cultures without which Rediscovery could never have come to be. But sharing traditions is not something which is taken lightly or comes about overnight. There is the duty of those passing on the tradition to see that it is passed on in the right way. Because of this, some sacred traditions which have been shared by native peoples through Rediscovery will never appear in a book. What we do offer in the following examples are opportunities for further exploring native cultures through a variety of activities — some with origins in native tradition and some which have evolved into distinct Rediscovery traditions of their own.

While the following activities are common to many Rediscovery camps, they are not suitable for all. Cultural sensitivity must be the guiding principle in their applications. For instance, Gambling Bones is widely practised by many native nations, but is sacred to some. At Wind River Rediscovery in Wyoming, the Arapahoe youth love to play it, but the Shoshone elders are upset by seeing it treated as a game and discourage it. Also offensive to some tribes is dressing in paints, masks, and robes, and using the feathers and fur of sacred animals in non-traditional ways. Consequently, Ceremony Night differs greatly from the dramatic theatrical traditions of the North Pacific coast to the American Southwest where regalia is inappropriate. In intertribal programs these restrictions can be difficult to work with; what one tribe takes lightly another considers most sacred. Above all in sharing traditions, it is important to share in sensitivity.

Four-Fire Ceremony

The Four-Fire Ceremony makes for a dramatic and symbolic opening to the first night of camp, emphasizing awareness of self, unity with the group, and oneness with the natural world.

Choose a site for the camp's council fire, and, using this as a central point of reference, prepare four small fire sites along the cardinal compass points, all radiating out equal distance from the centre. A beach, meadow, desert, or relatively open forest are all suitable locations for this activity as long as the fires are properly built and safely contained.

Divide the participants into four equal groups, give four sticks of wood to each person, and direct each group to their initial fire site. One staff member is appointed to each of the four "direction" fires while a fifth conducts the drumming from the council-fire site in the centre (still unlit). After spending five to ten minutes at each fire, all four groups rotate clockwise at the sound of the drum.

The fire guardians welcome each group to their directional fire by dramatically describing the aspects of that direction. Each of the four directions correspond with a different colour, element, and animal. The five guardians should reflect this by painting their faces in the colour of their direction and wearing a corresponding coloured blanket. For instance, a northern-fire guardian dressed in white robes and holding a large fan greets the group of youngsters with a blast of wind and the words:

"Welcome to the North. My element is air. I am the wind that fans the flames [do so], that sets the waves dancing across the water, causes the trees to sway and the snow to drift. My colour is white and my animal the buffalo. I am the home of the aurora borealis, the direction of winter darkness and summer light. I am the breath of the buffalo in the wintertime, the cold, strong, cleansing winds of the arctic, the shadow of the snowy owl that races across the treeless tundra and loses itself in the vastness. Offer the north fire one of your sticks and a quiet promise to become like it: strong as the buffalo, pure as the snow, and joyful as the aurora that dances in the night. Let us observe a moment of silence as our sticks brighten the flames and we each make our resolution."

After five to ten minutes of presentation and quiet reflection, the staff member at the central council-fire site begins drumming as the signal for all groups to rotate clockwise. This procedure is repeated for all directions:

"Welcome to the East. My element is fire and my colour red. I am the red glow before the dawn, the warmth of the morning sun as it falls on your face. I am the fire you see before you, energy from the sun absorbed by the trees, stored in the wood and now released to warm you here in the night. My animal is the eagle, free and majestic. Let your spirits too soar high each day as you face my direction and greet the sacred dawn."

"Welcome to the South. I am the earth. [The guardian holds up soil, sand, or rock in their hands]. My colour is yellow. I am the golden sands of the seashore and deserts. I am the body whose gravitational force draws objects toward me, the nurturing mother to which plants attach their roots. My animal is the coyote, the clever one, that roams the earth in search of fruit, rodents, and insects. Like you, my curiosity is never fully satisfied. My tracks crisscross the earth in quest of knowledge, and disappear on distant horizons."

"*Welcome to the West.* My colour is black and my element is water. I am the dark thunderclouds that sweep down out of the west and renew the earth with life-giving rain. [Sprinkle the participants with a few drops of water.] I have the power to douse fire [demonstrate]. Two-thirds of this planet is covered with me, ninety percent of your body is made of me, and life could not exist without me. My animal is the bear, strong and protective, that emerges from the darkness of the den to begin its life anew each spring. I am the black of night that enfolds us and without which we could not see the wonder of the stars."

Once each of the groups has visited all four direction fires and presented their sticks as offerings, the direction guardian and participants carry a torch from their fire and gather at the council-fire site. Drums and songs accompany the procession as all campers converge together. The staff member who has been stationed at the council-fire site, drumming throughout the ceremony, welcomes all to the centre of unity. The drummer wears all four colours on his or her face and the same colours on a blanket.

The wood of the council fire (prepared in advance) is now ignited with the flame of all four directions, as each torchbearer repeats the colour, element, and animal of their respective directions.

Once lit, the council fire may be blessed or dedicated by an elder or spiritual leader. The elder may choose to employ food offerings, smudgings (the burning of sage, cedar, or sweet grass and cleansing oneself with the smoke) songs, prayers, pipe ceremonies, or other culturally appropriate ceremonies. The council fire thus dedicated becomes a sacred site, the spiritual centre of the camp, the place for all to converge in a time of need. Harsh words must not be spoken here, nor the expression of ill will toward another. Garbage and cigarette butts must never be burned here. Many native people believe that there is a spirit that lives under the fire: one must always be careful not to offend.

Appropriate activities at the council-fire site include: the sharing of songs, legends, traditional dances; passing the eagle feather; Story Stick; the Solo vigil fire and closing Ceremony Night.

Native Crafts

What better way to share in the understanding of other cultures, or one's own, than by learning traditional skills and games. All Rediscovery programs put special emphasis on teaching native skills: basketry (spruce root, birch, and cedar bark); dance regalia (making masks,

Learning to make a skin drum requires many lessons: procuring a deer that offers itself up in a hunt, steaming the drum frame, fleshing and stretching the hide.

The completed drum is just the beginning of the learning process for a young Haida; drumming skills and proper songs must now be acquired and practised.

button blankets, moccasins, drums, bead and quill work); art (painting and carving argillite, soapstone, and wood); and others. These are not craft projects isolated from other events, but very much a part of daily camp life. For instance, a participant wanting to make a skin drum might find himself or herself arising before dawn for a ceremonial cleansing in the river prior to joining a skilled staff hunter on a food hunt. If a deer offers itself up, there is the necessary ceremony giving thanks. Packing the deer back to camp, gutting and skinning the carcass, stretching and fleshing the hide, are all part of the process. Then there's the drum frame to consider. A length of yellow cedar splits easily, but then comes the delicate and time-consuming task of planning and steaming the wood into a circular frame. Next comes stretching and lashing the wet hide over the frame, painting a design (if desired), and finally making a drumstick. The participant not only has a drum but has learned a dozen new skills in the process. But this is just the beginning. There are still songs to be learned, drumming skills to practise, and the elders to consult. In northwest coast cultures songs are property, and only certain songs can be sung, depending on one's lineage. Similarly, only certain crests could be used to decorate the drum. The Haida, Heiltsuk, Nuxalk, and Salish peoples have all been very generous in sharing many of these traditions with non-native staff and participants on Rediscovery.

Aside from crafts, traditional games, sleight of hand, and mind-twisters provide a fun way to share cultures. While it would be impossible to describe them all here, a few games will be outlined to demonstrate group dynamics, and the value such activities can have in stimulating cross-cultural appreciation.

Gambling Bones

Gambling Bones, or Lahal, is a native guessing game involving four players divided into two teams. Though there are variations from tribe to tribe, the game usually requires four bones, small enough to be concealed inside the closed palm of two players' hands. One bone in each player's hand is marked with a cut which the holder is able to feel. A set of eleven sticks is traditionally used as the gambling exchange item but on Rediscovery oranges, apples, wrapped popcorn balls, or other treats seem to inspire more total involvement on the part of the kids.

The teams of gamblers sit facing each other at close range, while their supporters gather alongside or behind. (Any number of supporters can join in.) An initial guess may determine which team will begin with the bones. If the two players on Team A win the bones, they will commence

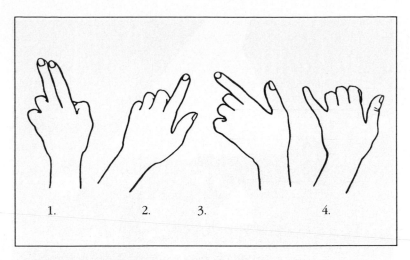

In Gambling Bones, one team member guesses the location of two unmarked bones, using hand signals.

a series of confusing hand movements and exchanges (behind their backs and in front), trying to confuse their opponents as to the location of the unmarked bones. Meanwhile, their supporters drum, and sing gambling songs in time with the hand movements, trying their best to distract the opposing team. When Team A is ready, the two players present their closed fists. One player is chosen from Team B to signal their guess. Two fingers laid down close together signals the two inner hands of Team A players (1). One finger to the right (2) or left (3) signals the corresponding hands of the two Team A players, and the extended thumb and little finger of the Team B player is used to signal the two outer hands of Team A (4). If the Team B player successfully guesses both marked bones, Team B now holds all the bones and challenges Team A to the guessing. If only one unmarked bone is guessed by Team B, then the Team A player holding the remaining unmarked bone continues playing. The Team B player who has not obtained an unmarked bone now guesses for the final bone. Each wrong guess throughout the game must be accompanied by payment to the opposite team of one of the treats (equally divided at the start between the two teams). Only when both marked bones are held by a team do they have an opportunity to win treats. The game ends when there are no longer treats to give out. Encourage the winning team to share the wealth of

Gambling Bones is a popular game with some native tribes and a sacred ritual with others. Cree youth play Gambling Bones at Wunskaw Wilderness Camp.

treats with the losers. Don't let the gambling go beyond the treat stage. There is a Haida story of a village so engaged in a gambling contest that with no material possessions left they gambled themselves into slavery.

Ring-On-A-String

Ring-on-a-String is a traditional game played in Bella Coola around a campfire circle. A small ring is suspended from a long circle of string held in the closed hands of all players. While the circle of players secretly pass the ring from hand to hand, one individual observes the movements from a standing position inside the circle. Facial expressions often tell the guesser more than the movement of the hands as circle members try to conceal their surprise when the ring is suddenly passed to them. All circle players move their hands along the string all the time, so guessing the ring's location can be very tricky. The circle of players may sing songs, change the direction of the ring, or try in other ways to distract those guessing. Sleight of hand and fake passes are the order of the day. The group can tease the guesser: "Let's all wave 'Hi!' to Johnny on the count of three: one, two, three, 'Hi Johnny!' " One-handed waves are easy, but two-handed are the worst tease of all. The person doing the

Birchbark cards depicting age-old symbols — loon's neck, lily roots, log over stream, two trails crossing, and others — are part of an ancient Thompson Indian game played on Stein Rediscovery.

guessing may be given a handful of apples, popcorn balls, cookies, or some other campfire snack which they must distribute, one to each individual, where they make a wrong guess. This helps to prevent careless and too-frequent guessings, and is an incentive to the circle players not to be careless in passing the ring. If a person gets caught with the ring they must enter the circle to become the new guesser. Any cookies, apples, or popcorn balls they have accumulated now go back to the general pot for redistribution. The game ends when all campfire treats have been distributed. If someone does not have a snack, the fortunate should be encouraged to share, in the same spirit they shared in the fun of the game.

This Is You

This Is You teaches players to not look beyond the obvious. The exact origin of this game remains a mystery, but it has become very popular with the Nuxalk and Haida at Rediscovery camps. Any group of people gathered around a table or sitting in a circle can play This Is You, as long as each individual can see every other. Five to six objects are placed on the table or at the centre of the circle. Anything will suffice: a spoon,

117

teacup, toothpick, flower, shoe, eyeglasses, a stone, pine cone, lighter, pack of matches, et cetera. The leader carefully arranges the objects in a seemingly meaningful way, assumes the same arm and hand posture as a person in the circle (John), and says: "This is you, John." All eyes will invariably be on the arranged objects and no one is likely to notice the mimic in posture. The leader now rearranges the objects, subtly assumes the arm and hand position of another person (Susan), and says with conviction: "This is you, Susan." As soon as someone catches on, they should be drawn into the game by having them arrange the objects and assume the posture of one in the group. "That's right," the leader can confirm, "that is Peter."

When more people learn how the game is played, the more maddening the situation becomes for those who are still bewildered. The game can go on for hours, which makes it a perfect indoor diversion during inclement weather. Generally, the casually observant character, rather than the analytical, intellectual type, figures out the game.

Goghits In The Woods

Every culture has mythological creatures, ghosts, goblins, witches, elves, and bogeys in countless variations. In Haida culture, Goghits (wild people of the forest), Slugus (land otters that take on human form), and Kuganas (evil spirits) are prominent in the mythology. Unlike most Caucasian cultures, where belief in spirit creatures is supposed to be restricted to childhood, some cultures retain belief in these forces throughout people's lives.

A Rediscovery group, hiking along the west coast with three Haida youth and two Caucasian children, once surprised a family of land otters returning to their den from the sea. The animals promptly hid themselves under a large boulder, while all five children dropped their backpacks at once. But while the white youth were scrambling for their "Instamatic" cameras, the Haida youth were biting their thumbs, covering their ears, and running in the opposite directions as fast as they could. When the Haida youth were safely a hundred feet away, they shouted back at the others in unison: "Get out of there, the Slugus will get you!" The white kids stared at them in bewilderment. Only later did they learn that Haidas believe land otters have the ability to take on human form and lead unsuspecting people deep into the forest with their hypnotic stare, persistent whistling, and supernatural powers. Hence the need to break the contact by biting the thumb, block the sound by covering the ears, and flee. If you do follow an otter into the forest, you are transformed into a Slugu yourself. The only way you can tell a Slugu in human form from a real person is to look for hair between their fingers and a cold nose. Because many of the parents and grandparents of Haida youth believe in Slugus, they become very real within the context of the culture. "Knowledge of these things breeds fear," Guujaaw, well-known Haida artisan, says; "the fear makes you pay attention."

Campfire legends are an excellent way to share legends and myths, but an activity like Goghits in the Woods creates spine-tingling, hair-raising, real-life Goghits. The activity is an all-time favourite on Haida Gwaii. It takes place at night, with one staff member telling a story about Goghits around the campfire. Goghits are legendary wild men in Haida culture, generally cast into the wild by boating mishaps and accompanying hypothermic conditions putting the person into a state of primal wild being. While one staff member captivates the participants with Goghit stories, the rest of the staff transform into Goghits — painting wild faces, ratting their hair, camouflaging themselves, and then hiding deep in the gloom of the forest. The storyteller uses considerable artistic licence in relating a make-believe story about children in the old days being sent off by their Haida nonnies (grandmothers) to pick wild rhubarb in the forest clearings. Their chini (grandfather) warns them that unless they return before dark, the Goghits in the woods might get them. "As long as you have some rhubarb or other food to offer the goghits, they will likely let you go," the grandfather cautions.

The leader gives each youngster three stalks of rhubarb from the camp garden, although any portable food item will do: apples, oranges, carrot or celery sticks. When all the participants have assembled at the edge of the forest, the storyteller has all the youth holler: "Are there any Goghits in there?" The bloodcurdling shrieks, howls, and growls from the hidden staff tell everyone they're in for a horrifying and hilarious experience.

Participants must get through the Goghit forest to a clearing or a line of survey ribbon strung along the back boundary. Here they can trade in each piece of rhubarb to a staff member for a fruit-and-nut candy bar. Every time a Goghit catches them either going in or returning, they must sacrifice a stick of rhubarb or one of their candy bars. Woe to the one who has nothing with which to appease the greedy Goghits. Capture is usually accompanied by play-wrestling and tickling, and more shrieks and growls.

In addition to providing an evening of silly fun, and learning about

A Haida Goghit master teaches apprentices the state of "primal wild being" in preparation for a ceremonial performance.

native myths, this game also bonds the staff and participants through uninhibited play.

A word of caution on safety. Because this activity takes place at twilight or in the dark, choose a location without a lot of unnecessary hazards, such as holes in the ground or sharp stems on trees.

Ceremony Night

Ancient drum songs emerge from the darkness while anxious eyes peer into the gloom of night in search of their source. Suddenly, burning torches appear like phantoms on the horizon, and an enormous eagle soars on thirty-foot wings. The youngsters huddled around the ceremonial bonfire draw even closer together. The drumming grows louder, supernatural beings approach — Raven with a long clacking beak, Grizzly Bear with fur and claws, and bare-chested warriors glistening with paint and oil in the light of their torches.

"Is Stoneribs coming, is he coming now?" There in the middle of the procession is one dressed in white robes, a scarlet sash, a crown of green hemlock branches, and a whale rib hoisted onto one shoulder. In the glow of firelight, a leader emerges and recites a direct translation of

120

Goghits in the Woods creates spine-tingling, hair-raising hilarity.

the ancient Haida legend:

"When Stoneribs came in he looked like a child of supernatural beings; he was dressed in a sacred manner. He went straight to the rear of the longhouse and he sat down under the wall of fire and received the flames. Soon he was burning inside; soon he was filled with fire — sparks floated out of him into the surrounding darkness. Supernatural beings shivered with fear."

There is nothing in the Rediscovery experience that can match the power and cultural drama of this final night of camp. Preparations for Feast and Ceremony Night begin during the expedition when each leader informs his or her group that they will be responsible for acting out a play. Whenever possible, these skits should be based on the traditional legends of the local indigenous culture. Costumes greatly enhance such performances, so it is a good idea to build up a collection of blankets, animal skins, dance masks, rattles, drums, and other regalia. Cedar, hemlock, and fir boughs make dramatic headbands and sashes, and many other natural objects (feathers, dry grass, seaweed, pine cones, seashells, et cetera) can be incorporated into costume making. Fish and Wildlife departments of government are usually good sources for obtaining animal furs and parts from specimens killed illegally or for scientific study. It is important for the camp staff to have a dress rehearsal with their performing group at the ceremony site sometime prior to the actual performance.

Much of the day is devoted to preparing a wild-foods feast for the closing banquet. On Haida Gwaii's Rediscovery this resembles a Haida potlatch (a gift-giving feast) in its preparations. Clams must be dug and steamed. Mussels and abalone are harvested from the rocks and prepared along with octopus and crab. Halibut, cod, salmon, and venison frequently find an honoured place at the banquet table. Fresh salad greens, potatoes, broccoli, cabbage, peas, and onions are harvested from the camp garden, along with strawberries and rhubarb for dessert. For an epicurean touch, wild berries and mushrooms are sought from the surrounding forest. Each participant is encouraged to work with a staff member to create a special gourmet item for the feast.

On Haida Gwaii's Rediscovery, where the traditions of Ceremony Night have had the longest to evolve, ritual is religiously observed. The dining hall is decorated with fresh cedar boughs, seashells, eagle feathers, animal masks, and dance blankets. Tablecloths, candles, and formal place settings with individual name tags remind everyone how special the event will be. Haida elders attending the feast do so in full ceremonial regalia — a custom normally reserved for honouring chiefs, weddings, and memorial feasts is here extended to honour the accomplishments of youth. Drum songs and a dinner blessing thanking the earth and sea for their rich bounty precedes the meal. Following dinner, each person takes a turn speaking of the time they've shared together. The warm family-like intimacy of the event lends itself well to full sharing.

As the banquet ends and darkness falls, faces are painted and costumes donned for the formal ceremony. One or two staff members accompany the participants to light the council fire, while the remaining staff secretly prepare for the Stoneribs procession. Torches for the procession are made with juice cans painted or burnt black, nailed to the top of wooden staffs, and stuffed with rags. Soaked in kerosene, the rags will burn safely for hours. A giant, fabric puppet kite in the shape of an eagle, bear, coyote, or other animal adds a powerful dimension to any procession. Garlands of cedar boughs and seashells strung between tall poles create an effective canopy above the group. A talking stick two to three metres long, carved or adorned with feathers, evergreens, shells, and bones, should be carried at the head of the procession. A leader announces at the council fire that during the formal presentations only the holder of the talking stick has the right to speak.

The formal part of the ceremony involves speeches acknowledging individual accomplishments, gift giving, and an opportunity for each participant to address the group. The drumming, singing, traditional dancing, and theatrical performances that follow run late into the night. For all, Ceremony Night marks not an end to the Rediscovery experience, but the celebration of a journey through life which has only just begun.

Medicine Wheel

A Medicine Wheel can be created at any point during a camp, but works especially well as a camp-closing ritual. Ask everyone in camp to collect a small natural object, and give some thought to what that object represents in terms of the group. (Pine cone, feather, flower, stone, leaf, twig, seashell, et cetera.) Now have the entire camp, participants, staff, cooks, volunteers, and guests gather and form a large circle: if possible, choose a location that is not used for other activities, so that the Medicine Wheel will not be disturbed.

A staff member can begin the ritual, explaining that each person will have an opportunity to leave behind something tangible, but totally natural, as a symbol of their feelings about the camp and each other. The staff member then walks to the middle of the circle and sets down his or her object: "This stone represents the permanence and strength of the bond of friendship we have formed here together."

The staff member returns to the outer circle, and the person to their immediate left goes to the centre. "This dead leaf symbolizes our departure, just as it too has separated from the tree."

The Medicine Wheel begins to grow, radiating outward like the petals of an opening flower as each new object is placed gently on the ground. "This feather reminds us of the song of the birds which greeted us here every dawn."

Water, air, and sunlight are less tangible but equally important elements someone may wish to add to the Wheel. (If a person is not quite ready to present their object and speak, move clockwise on to the next and work your way back around to them.) When everyone has placed their object and spoken, the Medicine Wheel is complete.

A friendship circle can be the perfect closing to the Medicine Wheel and the end of the camp session. It follows the exact same procedure as the Circle Greeting which opened the camp, but this time a friendly

Steamed crab on cedar boughs and salmon barbecuing around an open fire are part of the Haida Gwaii Rediscovery preparations for Feast and Ceremony Night.

The warm, family-like intimacy of a Stein Rediscovery Feast Night lends itself well to full group sharing.

embrace can replace the handshake. It should come as no surprise that even those participants too shy to shake hands on opening day are now embracing warmly.

SEEKING THE SPIRIT

These activities take a very personal approach to cultural awareness and appreciation by directly immersing youth in native ritual. Some of the activities have ancient origins, others come from new traditions now evolving at certain Rediscovery camps. All of them should be approached with reverence and respect. Native elders and spiritual leaders are often important in setting the tone for these pursuits, for although they involve group participation — they are intensely personal experiences — guidance is important.

Sunrise Ceremony

"In the life of the Indian there was only one inevitable duty, — the duty of prayer — the daily recognition of the Unseen and Eternal. His daily devotions were more necessary to him than daily food. He wakes at daybreak, puts on his moccasins and steps down to the water's edge.

Here he throws handfuls of clear, cold water into his face, or plunges in bodily. After the bath, he stands erect before the advancing dawn, facing the sun as it dances upon the horizon, and offers his unspoken orison. His mate may precede or follow him in his devotion, but never accompanies him. Each soul must meet the morning sun, the new sweet earth and the Great Silence alone!"

— Ohiyesa (Santee Dakota)

Native spiritual leaders at several Rediscovery camps encourage youngsters to rise at first light and quietly retreat in solitude to a location where the first rays of the rising sun will fall upon their face. At this sacred moment a silent prayer is offered: "Thank you, Grandfather [God, Great Spirit, Great Silence], for the gift of light — the gift of another day."

A Sunrise Ceremony can be an organized group event, but it becomes far more significant as an individual discipline. When a person begins each day spiritually connected to all life, their life becomes immeasurably enriched. Greeting the sun does not imply worship of it. Rediscovery leaders remind everyone that the sun is the source of energy for all life, that without its sustaining energy plants could not grow, water could not flow, and all life would soon perish.

Sacred Directions Run

Health and fitness are integral to every Rediscovery camp. A morning run not only provides for a good group activity to begin the day, but also helps build the strength, stamina, and personal discipline necessary for the five- to six-day backpacking, canoeing, or mountain-climbing expedition. An interesting cultural approach to the morning run, and one that provides moments of reflection, is the Sacred Directions Run.

The activity begins before breakfast, with the camp members gathered in a circle to perform twenty minutes of stretch exercises. Keep the talking to a minimum. This is not a disco-beat aerobics class with an over-energized instructor: try to set a reflective mood right from the start. Let each camper lead one exercise that all others imitate. Keep the energy moving around the circle.

The staff sets up the running course prior to the opening of camp, using a compass to flag a square course due north for one kilometre, then due east for another, due south for another, and finally due west back to a point not far from camp. Choose a beautiful site for each of the four resting points, and mark the location with a wooden staff or cairn decorated with coloured cloth. Eagle feathers, pine cones, seashells, and other natural objects can be added to these shrines by the campers. The coloured cloth designates the direction: white for north, red for east, yellow for south, and black for west. (These are the generally agreed upon sacred direction colours for many North American native tribes, though there are some exceptions.)

At the completion of the stretching exercises, set off in silence on the jog north. When all runners have arrived at the white marker, the entire group stands facing the shrine while one person recites from memory:

"This is the direction of North. Its colour is white.

It is where our European brothers and sisters come from.

It is the direction of pearly snow and glacial ice.

It is a direction of purity.

If you have any private thoughts or prayers, think about them now."

At first the staff will have to recite the words at each direction shrine, but by the third day participants should be familiar enough with the words assigned to this task. (Notify them which marker they will speak at before the run begins so they can prepare.)

A very short period of quiet reflection follows the presentation before the group runs on to the next direction. Each direction has its own presentation:

This is the direction of East. Its colour is red.

It is where our Indian brothers and sisters come from.

It is the sacred direction of the sunrise.

It is the new day that dawns and the light which fills the world.

This is the direction of South. Its colour is yellow.

It is where our Asian brothers and sisters come from.

It is the direction where the sun spends most of the day.

It is the life-giving, golden energy from the sun.

This is the direction of West. Its colour is black.

It is where our African brothers and sisters come from.

It is the direction of dark clouds and rain which cleanses the earth.

It is the black velvet which envelops the night.

Two further directions can be addressed, and for some native cultures it would be a sacrilege not to address them — the heavens and the earth. If there is a suitable place such as a dry meadow, or forest with dry moss, needles, or leaves, have everyone lie on their back, with eyes open wide, arms outstretched, and palms facing upward. One person recites:

Blue is the colour of the Above.

It is where the sun, the moon and the stars shine down on us.

It is the direction of light to which all plants grow.

Driftwood and cedar bark masks, as well as hemlock headbands and painted faces, are part of the regalia used on Haida Gwaii Ceremony Night.

A wolf dancer acts out a legend; a Haida girl's accomplishments are highlighted by her hike leader; and soloists are honoured at Stein Rediscovery — all part of Ceremony Night.

It is the thin blue atmosphere which envelops our living planet.

Now have everyone roll over face-first and turn the palms of their hands downward under their resting head, while one recites:

Green is the colour of the earth below us,

from which this rich soil nourishes the green forests.

It is the direction from which all plants grow and all life returns.

It is the green garment that adorns our living planet.

If you have any private thoughts or prayers, close your eyes and think about them now.

Allow the rest period at this final station to be a bit longer.

Morning Purification

The perfect follow-up to the Sacred Directions Run, Morning Purification turns everyone's cheeks rosy, an invigorating way to begin the day. Bathing at dawn in a glacial river, icy stream, or cold ocean may seem like an overly masochistic experience to the uninitiated, but it has ancient roots in native tradition. Haida strengthening ritual calls for immersing infants in the cold ocean every morning, thus increasing their survival time in the cold Pacific should a canoe swamp or capsize. Medicine people and spiritual leaders also used cold-water bathing as a form of self-discipline.

Morning Purification on Rediscovery can range from a mere dip in the ocean to cool off after a run to a much more formal and meaningful ritual. On Chako Kunamokst Rediscovery, youth completing the Sacred Directions Run dunk four times under the glacier-fed Dean River. They then scrub their bodies with fir boughs until their skin glows red and the needles begin to come off the branches. As one of the Nuxalk elders said: "You don't bathe in the icy creek at dawn to come in second."

Circle Hug

Circle Hug more properly belongs in Bonding, but it follows so naturally from the Sunrise Ceremony, Sacred Directions Run, and Morning Purification that it is included in this section on Seeking the Spirit. A Circle Hug, a simple variation of the Circle Greeting, uses hugs instead of mere handshake greetings. One person begins the hugging and each person follows in turn, moving clockwise around the inner perimeter of the circle of people. As they hug, each person wishes the other good morning.

In a society where fear of sexual connotations has virtually eliminated touch between teachers and students, parents and their offspring, many youngsters find themselves starved for that necessary human experience — healthy touch. Chako Kunanokst Rediscovery in Bella Coola has been very successful in helping troubled youth through daily Circle Hugs.

On the first morning of this activity, point out to the participants why hugging, like so many Rediscovery activities, succeeds best in a circle. Black Elk of the Oglala Sioux explained it eloquently:

"You have noticed that everything an Indian does is in a circle, and that is because the Power of the World always works in circles, and everything tries to be round. In the old days when we were a strong and happy people, all our powers came to us from the sacred hoop of the nation and so long as the hoop was unbroken the people flourished. The flowering tree was the living centre of the hoop, and the circle of the four quarters nourished it. The east gave peace and light, the south gave warmth, the west gave rain, and the north with its cold and mighty wind gave endurance. This knowledge came to us from the outer world with our religion. Everything the Power of the World does is done in a circle. The Sky is round and I have heard the earth is round like a ball and so are all the stars. The Wind, in its greatest power, whirls. Birds make their nests in circles, for theirs is the same religion as ours. The sun comes forth and goes down again in a circle. The moon does the same, and both are round.

"Even the seasons form a great circle in their changing, and always come back again to where they were. The life of a man is a circle from childhood to childhood and so it is in everything where power moves. Our tipis were round like the nests of birds and these were always set in a circle, the nation's hoop, a nest of many nests where the Great Spirit meant for us to hatch our children."

Talking To The Trees

Native peoples consider trees to have strong healing powers. Native women still pray to the cedar tree before removing bark to weave hats, baskets, or make medicine.

"Look at me friend
I come to ask for your garment
You always take pity on us
for there is nothing for which you cannot be used
because it is your way
that there is nothing for which we cannot use you,
For you are really willing to give us your garment.
I come to beg you for this

Talking to the Trees is an introspective exercise with roots in native tradition.

> Long Life Maker, Healing Woman, Supernatural One
> For I am going to make a basket for berries out of you.
> I pray friend, to tell your friends about what I ask you
> Take care friend
> Keep sickness away from me Healing Woman,
> Long Life Maker"
> *"Kwakiutl Prayer to Cedar Tree"*

For native people, trees came to symbolize the sacredness of all life, and they rested beside them with a feeling of being close to a mothering power. The Northwest Coast natives believed that one's longevity could be increased by leaning against an ancient cedar tree. Twelve-hundred-year-old cedars can still be found living on this coast.

Talking to the Trees is an introspective exercise that helps youngsters gain insight into the relationship with the land that all our ancestors once knew. This activity can take place any time of the day, but it will require some preparation on the part of the staff to set the right mood.

There are many poems and writings about trees and forests that the staff can read or recite to help set the mood. Example:

"You don't bathe in the icy creek at dawn to come in second."

"Trees seem to do their feats so effortlessly. Every year a given tree creates absolutely from scratch ninety-nine percent of its living parts. Water lifting up tree trunks can climb one hundred and fifty feet an hour; in full summer a tree can, and does, heave a ton of water every day. A big elm in a single season might make as many as six million leaves, wholly intricate, without budging an inch; I couldn't make one."
— Annie Dillard, from *Pilgrim at Tinker Creek*

Have the participants spread out through the forest so that no one is in view of another. When each finds a tree they like, they should sit down and lean against it, or embrace it standing. Some will find it easier to talk with their eyes closed. Trees are good listeners and can keep secrets forever, so there is no need to be shy.

To enhance this experience for the sceptic, take a stethoscope and position the youngster at a tree with thin bark. By listening carefully, one can hear the sap being drawn upward, much like a human heartbeat. (This is especially pronounced in the springtime.) Leave the child to listen to the heartbeat of the tree as well as their own. Words at this point may not be necessary at all.

The staff can never know whether or not any given participant actually found something to say to their tree, unless they feel like sharing their experience with others. Some may be more comfortable writing a poem or relating their feelings in their journals. Encourage them to take them along. One boy wrote:

Tall trees stretch to the sky
While in their shadows the fallen empire lies to rot
Cool, dark and dim, the forest is alive
Green boughs match green moss
Red cedar matches red earth
The thousand year children reign today
And topple tomorrow

CHAPTER 3
THE WORLD AROUND US

In the soft half-light of a coastal rainforest, surrounded by cool moist moss, six youngsters sit in silence, listening intently to the hushed voice of a native elder. A spruce needle is held aloft between the weathered fingers of the elder. "Now watch closely, smell strongly, and listen carefully," the elder whispers. From somewhere deep in the forest a varied thrush sings a long lonely note. A sea breeze stirs the forest canopy and a light shower of needles falls quietly to the moss-carpeted forest floor. Suddenly, the elder no longer holds the spruce needle. "Did you see it? Did you smell it? Did you hear it?" the elder asks. The youngsters appear puzzled. The lesson is repeated. This time a few kids catch the release of the needle and watch its soundless descent to the ground. The elder looks up to the treetops sixty metres overhead, then deep into the eyes of the youngsters. The elder speaks slowly: "When a spruce needle falls in the forest the eagle sees it, the bear smells it, and the deer hears it." The lesson is effective and simple. Eagles have seeing powers ten times better than humans, bears' noses far outpower our own, and look at those big radar receptors on deer. Now it's time for some forest games: "Eagle eyes, Bear nose, Deer ears."

An old adage declares: "I hear and I forget; I see and I remember; I do, I touch, and I understand." Native North Americans employed the same principle to teach their youth for generations prior to the introduction of European school systems. Even today, traditional native teachers do not lecture or assign a book to read, but teach by example. Amongst natives, you would seldom hear the question: "Can you teach me how to do that?" More often than not, silent immediate immersion in the activity is shared by the doer and the watcher. A native girl watches her grandmother fillet many salmon for barbecuing before attempting it herself. When the untrained hand finally puts the knife to the fish, experience borne from close observation makes the task simpler, faster, and cleaner. "Do as I do" does not need to be spoken.

In the same manner, a child might watch many carvers manipulating the different tools with a variety of approaches to their final product. The child might witness the moulding of a dozen different mediums and artistic styles before trying their hand, and, if it is their interest, developing their own style.

Rediscovery recognizes that not all knowledge is taught in the same school. Nature itself provides the best university for learning, but often our senses must be reawakened first. By teaching environmental principles within an experiential framework, Rediscovery not only rekindles a childlike sense of wonder in the natural world, it allows for much deeper understanding of it. The following activities are designed for group sharing; they are divided into six categories for easy reference: Exploring, Sensing, Connecting, Communicating, Surviving, and Tuning In.

EXPLORING

All the activities here are exploring in a new way, taking time to really look close, examine, and absorb. They help youngsters to travel over a landscape and make it new again — to feel like the first person to ever set foot in a place, or to see it in a way that no one else has ever seen it! Photographing the intricacy of a spider web with a blink of the eye; probing the hidden recesses of a tide pool with sensitive fingers; fathoming the vastness of the universe on an imaginary space journey; or discovering the silent mysteries of the night world — exploring helps us to step off the path, to travel with the imagination and senses wide open.

Camera Kids

As any nature photographer can attest, cameras can be an effective

A Haida master carver silently shares his skills with a Rediscovery participant.

tool for putting people in more intimate contact with the natural world. Close-up lenses help us peer closely into nature's intricacies and beauty. Camera Kids literally opens eyes to nature, with no camera at all. First, pass around a few good nature photos, and ask some questions: "Did the photographer take a close-up or a distance shot? horizontal or vertical? with the light behind or in front of the camera? with the main subject in the centre or off to one side? Which photos do you like best? How long do you think this photographer had to wait until the spider crawled to the edge of its web?" Now have everyone find a partner and decide which in each pair will be the photographer and which will be the camera. Demonstrate how a human camera works by gently holding the sides of the head of a partner from behind. "Now, as in all good cameras the shutter stays closed [close your partner's eyes]. To open the shutter and take a picture, you simply push one of your partner's ear lobes while saying 'click' and close it by releasing the ear lobe with another 'click'. This motion opens and closes the eyes for the desired exposure length — usually one to two seconds. At all other times the camera's eyes are closed."

Once everyone has mastered the technique, ask them to go off with their camera and photograph the three most beautiful images they can find. Flowers, ferns, moss, and tree bark all make for wonderful close-ups by positioning your camera partner's head directly over the object before releasing the ear lobe shutter. Panning shots of landscapes, treetops, creeks, and ocean vistas can also be shot video style, with a three- to four-second time exposure. A creative photographer might wish to photograph the leaves floating on a rain puddle with the reflection of the camera and photographer looking back at the lens from the water. As in real photography, creativity, composition, and lighting are the keys to good images.

Once a photographer has completed the three assigned photos, they become the camera, and their partner leads them off on a photo session.

As soon as each team returns, having completed their assignment, hand out blank index cards and coloured pencils or pens, so that each camera can process the one image in their mind they liked best. The photographers should not view the pictures as their camera is processing.

When everyone has finished their drawings, gather the entire group in a circle and begin passing all the images clockwise for everyone to have a look. On the second rotation of the images, ask the photographers to pull out the image that they took (the one their camera

138

processed). It is interesting to see if a photographer can recognize their own work as interpreted by another.

As a nice closing to this exercise, have the cameras autograph their photo and dedicate it to their photographer, *"With love, your camera"*, before presenting it as a memento.

Lost Planet

Lost Planet is ideal for a close examination of a sphagnum bog, alpine meadow, tundra, or a rock face adorned with mosses and lichens.

"Ahhh, here we are deep in the heart of the bog — what a weird-looking place. Doesn't it seem like we're on some kind of lost planet? Look at the strange shapes of those dwarf trees and this unearthly red and orange moss. Oh oh, look out! Watch where you step," the instructor warns. "There's animal-eating plants living here."

Give out space explorer kits to all participants and ask them to spread out in search of a Lost Planet. The kits contain a one-metre length of survey tape, a jeweller's lens, and seven toothpick flags.

Once the space explorers locate their Lost Planet, they define its boundaries with the survey ribbon and study the world carefully for signs of life or other unique features, planting a flag to mark each of the seven wonders of that particular world. Space explorers should invite one another to their planets and together tour the Seven Wonders of their World with the aid of their jeweller's lens. "The first wonder on my planet is the dark hole of the mighty centipede: there's the pine-needle steps for its hundred legs." The space explorer points to the next toothpick flag, "you'll need the lens to see the second wonder. See the drops hanging on the moss. They're like giant diamonds on this planet." Young children generally use far more imagination on this exercise than teens or adults.

Staff members should also take tours of each of the youngster's Lost Planets and ask questions to get them thinking: "Why do you suppose the plants on this planet have hairy leaves and stems? Do you think this planet is very dry? windy? What is its atmosphere like? How cold do you think it gets here? How do the plants on your planet reproduce? What eats them?" The questions can lead into complexities such as the high acidity of a bog, the short growing season of the alpine and tundra, wind desiccation, the role of lichen in breaking down rocks and absorbing nitrogen directly from the air. Don't dwell on the lessons. The main purpose of Lost Planet is to open one's eyes to the natural world — especially the micro-world we rarely take notice of.

"Click!," a Camera Kid imprints the image of a wildflower in his mind as his photographer touches an earlobe to open his eyes.

The Conundrum Hunt

"This is a conundrum plant," the leader points out as the group follows the trail through the woods to camp. Everyone continues walking, and, a little farther along, the leader stops the group and points to a different plant. "This is a conundrum plant." "A what?" asks one of the hikers. "A conundrum plant." "But I thought you said that other short plant was a ... you-know plant." "You don't have a very good memory," says the leader, and points to a third type of plant. "This is the conundrum." "Hey," say several hikers, "that's a different one." The leader shakes her head and says, "I think we'd better sit down and figure this out."

The leader then points to several plants and trees, asking the name of each. Some shout out the correct names. Others make wild guesses. "What do the names tell us about these plants? What if I called this one Joe and this one Jill? We know they have different names, that they are different, but we don't know how. If I call this a conundrum plant, all you know is its name, which is easy to forget. You don't know that you can eat the berries or that the leaves stay green all year. It's good to learn

140

Deep in the heart of a sphagnum bog, a boy discovers the seven wonders of his world in Lost Planet.

the names of plants and animals, but it's more important to learn what makes each one different from the others: how they fit into the forest." The leader pulls some paper from her pack. "Actually *these* are conundrums — questions like riddles that will make you think about the connections between everything here in the forest." The leader hands out the lists. "Once you've figured out the conundrum, you have to search for the thing and bring it back."

All that's required to make a conundrum list educational as well as experiential is to use imagination in listing the items everyone will hunt for. For instance, instead of listing "a piece of birchbark," the conundrum list might read "the bark of a tree which can be used to make baskets, canoes, writing paper, and good fire starter." Instead of listing a "sundew plant" in the bog, the list could read "a piece of a plant that eats animals." Conversely, a deer hair or dropping could read "a piece of an animal that eats plants." The important thing here is to require the participants to focus on the relationships between living things more than the names of the objects they collect. Stress beforehand that only small pieces of plants should be collected, and that the environment where the activity takes place should be damaged as little as possible.

A metamorphic rock could be listed as "a piece of something formed under intense heat and pressure." A dab of mud might be listed as "a piece of something which could turn to shale under intense pressure." One listing that always brings interesting results is "something which has no value in nature." Many youngsters will bring back dead leaves, twigs, or stones for this item. Explain to them how everything in nature has value.

Conundrum Hunts can be done individually, in pairs, or small groupings. The important thing is not so much what is collected as the process of searching, touching, differentiating, and understanding. A list of twelve to twenty objects will keep a group occupied for an hour or more. Small plastic ziplock bags make good collecting bags, and bug boxes are good additions when insects are involved. Be sure the students release the insects alive and undamaged at the completion of the exercise.

A typical conundrum list might read as follows: (correct items are listed in brackets)

— Something squirrels like to eat (acorns, pine cones, mushrooms)
— Something small that preys on birds and mammals (mosquito, deer fly, blackfly)
— A modified scale used for flying (bird feather)

— A tree bark natives used for making baskets (cedar, birch, ash)
— A bark that breaks off smooth and round like a fish scale (spruce)
— Something that has passed through a digestive tract (any type of animal dropping)
— Something sticky that is good for starting fires, healing cuts and as chewing gum (spruce pitch)
— Three different things that convert sunlight to sugar (needles, leaves, moss)
— A plant that fixes nitrogen directly from the air (lichen)
— Something that all life requires (water, air, sunlight)
— Something that has no value in the forest (nothing naturally present)

Greet A Tree

"Which two people in our group look the most alike?" the hike leader suddenly asks, as a group of youngsters stop to rest in the forest. There is a lot of looking back and forth before everyone realizes there really aren't many similarities. "Well, no two trees in the forest look any more alike than any two individuals in your group," the leader proclaims. "Let's have a look." Take some time to compare differences in bark texture, girth, trunk configuration, height and limb structure, even between trees of the same species. Now have the group divide into pairs, and, while one in each party is being blindfolded with a kerchief, the instructor comments: "There is a tree in this forest that has been waiting to meet you all its life, and it is much, much older than you. The tree is a little shy about this first encounter," the guide explains, "so we are having your friend lead you there blindfolded. When you greet your tree for the first time, touch it gently. Feel how strong it is. Touch its bark and limbs. See if you can wrap your arms around its trunk. Get to know your tree as best you can, because you will need to find each other later."

The participants set off in pairs. The guide for each blindfolded youngster should hold one of their partner's hands extended out in front and have their other hand reassuringly rested on their partner's shoulder. Youngsters love this part of the exercise, though there can be a tendency to abuse the privilege by leading the blindfolded into a lot of unnecessary obstacles. Remind everyone that they will be exchanging positions at some point, so they will want to do unto their partner as they would have that person do unto them.

Once a blindfolded participant has had some time alone with their tree and comes to know it well by touch, they are then led (rather

A stalk of cotton grass is collected as a possible "seed with angel's wings" on a Conundrum Hunt.

A blindfolded youngster is carefully led by her partner to Greet A Tree.

indirectly) back to the place where they started from. The blindfold is removed, and the youngster is asked to find and greet their tree again.

Most participants will be able to locate their tree from memory, but occasionally a person becomes extremely disoriented and searches in vain. Have their partner give them clues such as "you're getting warmer [colder]" until they and their tree are successfully reunited.

Some youngsters become so attached to their tree that they seek it out again and again during the course of the program. A distressed camper that runs off to be alone for some particular reason can often be found at the base of their tree, as can a camper who doesn't want to leave on the day of departure.

Bigfoot

Everyone has heard the tales of Sasquatch or Bigfoot, the large apelike creature believed by some to inhabit North America's Pacific Northwest. Let all the participants imagine themselves to be a Sasquatch. Give them each a notepad and pen, a magnifying glass, and a coat hanger bent into the shape of a Sasquatch footprint. Then invite them to spread out in any direction they choose, taking giant Bigfoot steps as they go. Before everyone gets too far apart, the instructor shouts: "Stop, Bigfoot!"

Now all the players are instructed to squat down beside the spot where their next footstep would have been and mark it by carefully setting down their Bigfoot step. Then they take out their pen, paper, and magnifying glass, and record as many different things as they can find: cones, needles, seeds, twigs, flowers, leaves, spiders, ants, mushrooms, lichens, liverworts .... If the participants don't know the names for all the items, they should try to describe them as best they can. The instructor should also rotate from site to site, pointing out details and interesting features of the forest floor the students wouldn't otherwise be aware of. Examples: "Look here, you have a centipede crawling into your Bigfoot step. Notice the black and yellow colouration. That's a warning signal to birds. *Don't eat me, I taste awful!* Pick up the centipede and smell it to get some idea of how it might taste. And look, over here, near your Bigfoot toe you have a lichen, one of the oldest plants on the planet. It is actually two plants appearing as one — a partnership between algae and fungus. A relationship that's good for both parties is called symbiosis."

Groups may spend thirty to fifty minutes engrossed in a world they normally walk over quickly. A list of forty items or more is not uncommon in an old-growth forest, much less in second-growth sites.

146

The activity Octopus Garden needs a low tide when rich and colourful tide pools are exposed.

"Don't look now, just touch," an instructor encourages a boy feeling
a moon snail shrinking back into its shell.

148

Exploring every nook and cranny of an Octopus Garden with one's fingers can bring many discoveries, including a baby octopus.

Once all the surface of a Bigfoot step has been surveyed, invite the participants to look a few centimetres underground for a whole list of objects: soil, roots, mould, centipedes, worms, mites, ant and spider eggs, et cetera. Encourage everyone to put their nose down under the ground and have a deep smell of good, clean earth. "Just think," the instructor concludes, "most of the creatures that live in the temperate forests, live here underground — but our magnifying lenses aren't powerful enough to see them."

Because Sasquatches don't like their whereabouts known, it is important to conceal all signs of one's Bigfoot step before leaving the site.

Wanted Dead or Alive, found in the Connecting section, is designed to follow Bigfoot.

Octopus Garden

Ocean covers three-quarters of our planet, yet few youngsters ever peer closely into this amazing living realm. Octopus Garden needs a low tide when rich and colourful tide pools are exposed along rocky shores. Because tide pools never dry up, the animals and plants found there are

149

those normally only visible much lower in the tide zone. Explain that while only a large tide pool can support an octopus, even the small ones contain most of the same plants and animals of an octopus garden.

Give each youngster "octopus eyes," a twelve-inch length of plastic pipe with Plexiglas (or a magnifying lens) sealed onto the end. Moving ever so slowly through the water so as not to frighten the tide pool dwellers, have them stalk the starfish, limpets, chitons, hermit crabs, sculpins, nudibranchs, and flowerlike anemones. They should explore every nook and cranny of their Octopus Garden with their periscope, then repeat the experience with their fingers.

"Don't look now, just touch," the instructor encourages. "Nothing in your garden can hurt you. Even the sharp spines of the sea urchin don't hurt you if you touch them very gently. Watch how the tentacles of a sea anemone draw towards the mouth when you touch them. The sticky feeling you get when you touch these tentacles is thousands of little stinging darts entering your fingertips. That's how anemones capture their prey [small fish, crabs, or snails], but they can't hurt you. Ever so slowly, move your fingers along the bottom like an octopus. You are feeling with five fingers. Imagine how much more an octopus senses with eight arms."

Octopus Garden is followed by Tide Pool Community, which is described in the Connecting section. This exercise can also be easily adapted to a pond or lake shore by changing the name and focus.

Night Safari

Few youngsters realize there are as many creatures that inhabit the world of darkness as inhabit the daylight. Night Safari is an adventure into the little-explored shady side of the earth.

To prepare for Night Safari, blacken everyone's hands and face with burnt cork. All explorers should wear dark clothing, long-sleeved shirts, and long pants. (Try not to use insect repellent.) Rub fir branches on the back of the neck and over one's clothing to help disguise human scent. It won't take long before the campers get excited about the prospects of wildlife sightings in the dark, and fully understand the need for camouflage.

Set the mood for the evening by talking in a hushed voice about some of the nocturnal wildlife the group might encounter: deer, raccoon, mice, skunks, bats, owls, rabbits, coyotes. The possibilities, of course, will vary with each area. The forest provides an ideal setting for a Night Safari because of the intensified darkness, but desert, tundra, and wild

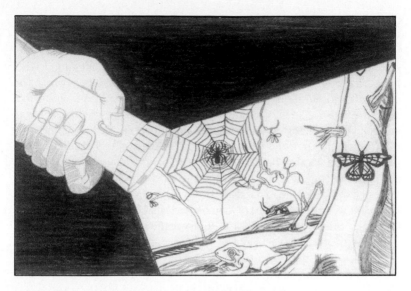

Night Safari *by Rediscovery participant Leon Ridley.*

meadows are also suitable during the dark phases of the moon.

Take a bright flashlight on the safari only for emergency. Let the group learn to improve their night vision, entering the forest just as darkness fully descends, and slowly adjusting to the reduced light. Total darkness does not exist even in the deep gloom of the forest at night. Have everyone look up to realize that they can still draw the outline of the treetops against the sky with their fingertips.

Now have the participants move as far away from the instructor as they feel comfortable doing. Explain that the best chance of viewing night creatures will come to those who remain perfectly still, and that the farther spread out the group becomes, the better the opportunities for sightings. Everyone must understand that any unnecessary movement or noise on their part will spoil the experience for the entire group.

The instructor should choose a location where animals are known to frequent, a natural salt lick, watering hole, deer trail, grazing location, den site, or owl tree. If the participants become impatient and appear fidgety after a while (fifteen to twenty minutes), light a candle as the signal for them to all come back together. Have everyone share their secret sightings in a soft whisper. Ask if anyone felt fearful or even uncomfortable being in the dark alone. Ask too if anyone overcame some of their fear of the dark during the exercise.

Even if no wildlife sightings turned up during the solo session, the next activity will surely uncover some. Turn everyone's attention to the little creatures of the night, the mice, shrews, frogs, and others who have evolved to locate their prey, avoid predation, or attract a mate in the dark: the bat's sonar; the owl and deer's superb hearing; the frog, cricket, and katydid's singing; and the firefly's illumination. "Let's become one of those creatures, while we explore," the instructor says excitedly. Tiny penlights are handed out to all the participants. "You are all fireflies," the guide tells the group. "Spread out wherever you like and use your light to explore for life in the dark. If you discover something interesting you want to share with others, don't speak, just blink your light on and off, like a firefly, as a signal for them to come to you."

This is an absorbing activity which can go on late into the night. If the sky is clear and there is a clearing nearby, Stargazers makes a perfect close to the Night Safari.

Stargazers

Ironically, in our age of space travel, today's youth are further removed and less knowledgeable about the stars and constellations than the average shepherd thousands of years before the time of Christ. Even when students take an active interest in the stars, their illuminated urban environments usually eliminate any possibility of serious observation. It is important, therefore, that youth camps set aside time for stargazing even if it means extending the usual bedtime.

Stargazers can open eyes to the infinite universe. All that's needed is a clear night, a dark and open viewing location (like a large meadow, open hilltop, beach, or lake edge), a few blankets, and some willing stargazers.

Have everyone lie on their backs on the blankets, with eyes closed, heads touching, and hands clasped with those beside them. "Is everyone ready for a space journey?" the instructor asks. "Okay, close your eyes and prepare to lift off." Pre-teens love the countdown to takeoff. Shortly after ignition and blastoff, when the vibrating arms and legs calm down, give the signal to open the ship's viewing windows. With all eyes peering into the sky, the instructor advises: "Now hold on tight, because we are hurling through space at an incredible 65,000 miles per hour aboard our spaceship *Earth*. The light that's reaching our eyes now was sent out from the nearest star more than four years ago. Can you find the brightest star in the sky? Yes, that's it, Sirius to the south. [Point to it.] It's nearly nine light years away. Some of the stars we see tonight may not even exist any more. They are so far away that the light we see from them now was sent out during the time of the dinosaurs.

"Can anyone see the centre of our galaxy? Yes, that's it — that beautiful band of light, the Milky Way. Here we are, a little planet in a solar system on the edge of this vast galaxy. Billions of stars burn brightly in our galaxy, but even on the clearest nights our eyes can only see about two thousand stars in the entire sky. How incredible to know that beyond this galaxy are others like it — and on and on to an infinity we cannot even imagine."

As the evening unfolds, the instructor may want to help the youngsters identify various constellations, determine the phase of the moon, talk about the gravitational influence of the sun and the moon, and search for shooting stars and satellites. This opportunity to interest the participants in astronomy may be unparalleled in a student's life. Celestial navigation and direction-finding can also be discussed. It is not unusual for a group to spend an hour or more in this relaxing and absorbing experience. The intimacy with the group through heads and hands touching can bring on some very personal sharing. Let each person in the stargazing circle have an opportunity to speak and share their feelings by sending a hand squeeze to the person beside them once they themselves have finished speaking.

SENSING

Sensing activities take us beyond the borders of our everyday sight, hearing, smell, taste, and touch — giving us, for an imaginary moment, the powers of creatures with senses far more developed than our own. What does it feel like to smell with a bear's nose, see with an eagle's eyes, hear with a deer's ears? By singling out one of our five senses and focusing our energy on it, we can become receptive to the natural world in ways we never imagined.

There is a sixth sense at work in these activities, the ability to perceive, feel, or be conscious of a thing or place. Blindfolded youngsters do a snail crawl in a forest back to the spot where they believe they were first blindfolded. Many are successful. A child responds to an insect with black and yellow colouration. The child senses danger, although in this case it's only a fly mimicking a bee to avoid predators. As in the animal world, the awareness of all six senses is important in human development.

Eagle Eyes

Eagles, like most raptors, have extraordinary vision. An object rarely visible to the human eye at thirty-three metres is still visible to a falcon or eagle at three hundred and sixty metres. A raptor's eye does not magnify so much as provide for incredible distance perception.

To see for yourself how good an eagle's eyes can be, use a thread spool or other bright object about 3 centimetres long. Place the spool on the ground and have each youngster start backing away from it. When each kid can no longer see the spool they have reached the limits of their eyes' resolving power. Measure the distance and multiply it by ten and you will know how much farther away an eagle could be and still see the spool.

Another way to illustrate the difference between human and eagle eyes is to use 10-x-25 or 10-x-50 binoculars to increase human distance perception tenfold.

It is best to experience Eagle Eyes from a high perch — a pinnacle, hilltop, or even a large tree platform that can safely support four to six viewers. On Haida Gwaii's Rediscovery, participants are able to look down into two active eagle nests from their pinnacle perch. Not all settings, however, are so richly endowed.

To begin the exercise, have the youngsters imagine themselves eagles sitting high above ground in a huge nest of sticks. The instructor should point out some of the fascinating features of eagle nests:

"Here we are more than thirty metres above ground, sitting in an enormous eagle nest. A typical nest could easily hold three or four of us, and some nests have been recorded as being four metres deep and seven metres across, and weighing more than seven tonnes! Records show bald eagles occupying the same nest continuously for more than one hundred years. Of course, that means many generations of eagles being raised in the same nest.

"This nest platform and nearby perch trees are important to us for another reason," the instructor continues. "Imagine if we had to always be flying in search of everything we ate. We'd likely be expending more energy than our food would replenish. That's why eagles always build their nests and have their perch trees near many food sources. Let's see what possible foods we can spot with the aid of our Eagle Eyes."

Everyone becomes alert for any movement or sign of food below them. Pass the binoculars from one youngster to the next, allowing each the power of Eagle Eyes. Now that everyone is experienced with the binoculars, see how many tiny markers they can spot in the surrounding

Eagle Eyes *by Rediscovery participant Leon Ridley.*

area — small index cards with an eagle's food drawn on each card: rabbit, deer, mouse, duck, salmon, seal, sea lion, seagull, crab, or abalone. They must be set out by the instructor beforehand, along the shoreline, in an open meadow, or tied to branches where appropriate. All markers must be clearly visible from the viewing perch but small enough to be legible only with the aid of the binoculars. Now it's time for a guessing game of "I Spy."

The first participant to look through the binoculars scans the surrounding area, then says, "I spy with my Eagle Eyes something for an eagle to eat that is pink." The binoculars go around the circle, each

*"I spy with my Eagle Eyes something for an eagle to eat that is shiny,"
a girl proclaims from her perch.*

person trying to spot the eagle food. After one person passes the
binoculars to the next person, they try to guess, using only yes or no
questions. Some questions might be: "Is it in the ocean?" "Can it hide
under a huckleberry bush?" "Does it move quickly?" If the binoculars
go all the way around, with no one guessing correctly, then they all get
one more guess, and maybe someone will say, "Is it the abalone down
at the low tide line?" The correct guesser gets to do the next "I spy with
my Eagle Eyes." Three's A Crowd, in the Connecting section, is a good
follow-up to Eagle Eyes.

Bear Nose

Just look how well-developed bears' noses are compared to their tiny,
close-set eyes. The old song "the bear went over the mountain to see
what he could see" is, for the most part, nonsense. Bears are notoriously
near-sighted. More likely, the bear went over the mountain to see what
he could smell from many miles away.

Bear Nose helps youngsters appreciate the importance of smell,
especially in animals who rely heavily on that sense.

Have participants take turns using their hands to cover each other's

A misplaced step, or crack of a twig underfoot, could mean game over for a predator stalking his quarry in Deer Ears.

eyes from behind while an instructor holds a forest object under someone's nose for sniffing. Once the person acknowledges that they have the scent firmly etched on their mind, hide the sample and tell the helper to uncover the participant's eyes. The sniffer must now find that exact same scent in the area and bring a small sample back to the instructor. A lot of sniffing later, the participant should return with the correct smell item. Should they fail, keep giving them a smell clue until they succeed.

Forest smells particularly good for Bear Nose are: mushroom or fungus, rotten wood, tree pitch, evergreen needles, dry leaves, liverwort, animal droppings, wild berries, aromatic roots, and small samples of understory plants. (Try to avoid using wildflowers, as so many are becoming endangered.) The more subtle the smell, the more challenging the exercise. Crush the objects before presenting them for sniffing, to release the full aroma. The more subtle smells must be held very close to the nose, but be careful not to allow the object to touch any part of the face, or else a non-smell clue will be involved. The instructor must also take care to keep his or her hands as free of previous scents as possible. Don't put spruce pitch on one's finger, or every bear will return with the same strong-smelling object.

After the exercise, discuss which of the smell objects gathered a bear might actually eat. Encourage the youngsters to taste any that are also edible for humans.

Deer Ears

Choose a quiet forest setting for Deer Ears, away from roads, loud creeks, or surf and with plenty of forest litter. "Have you ever wondered why a deer's ears are so big?" the instructor asks.

Have each person cup their hands behind their ears to simulate a deer's. Without changing his or her tone of voice, the instructor asks, "How many think I'm speaking louder now?" The apparent change in volume is fairly dramatic.

"Let's demonstrate just how important a deer's hearing is," the instructor continues. "We're going to play a game called Deer Ears. One of you will be blindfolded and will kneel here in the forest like a deer grazing at night. The rest of you will become predators: wolves or cougars. The predators must start the game at least fifteen metres away from the deer. When I give the signal to start stalking, you must slowly and silently begin pursuing your prey. If the predators get close enough to the deer to snatch a cloth 'tail' from the deer's back pocket, then the deer is dead. But if the deer hears you coming and points in your direction, saying, "Starve!," then you're out of the game."

Now a deer can't be so paranoid that it stops eating and flees with every little movement it hears, or it would probably starve itself. So to make the situation more realistic the deer will only be able to point and shout *Starve* as many times as there are predators (plus two extra).

A staff member will have to monitor the game closely and be certain that all players stop stalking every time the deer says "Starve!" If the deer points within two or three degrees of a predator, that person is out of the game and must now sit in total silence. (It is best to have each person caught sit quietly beside the instructor.) The instructor can then give the "Continue stalking" go-ahead to those predators still in the game.

There is great suspense as the wolves and cougars creep closer to the deer. The successful predators are those who make their advances while the deer is distracted in another direction. The successful deer are constantly alert to sound from any direction, frequently moving their [hand-cupped] ears in different directions just like real deer, and periodically altering their grazing position. Be sure to keep the deer's ears exposed when tying the blindfold: a set of antlers tied to the head

"Imagine yourself as a snail, moving ever so slowly across the landscape."

of the deer adds a realistic touch to the game and seems to assist in the role-play.

Let the person who kills the deer become the next deer. This game is so popular with youngsters that everyone in the group will want a turn playing deer. Following the exercise, take a moment to discuss other adaptations deer have to avoid predation, such as long necks, and eyes on the sides of their heads, which allows them to see in every direction except right behind them. Speed and agility are other defence strategies. Discuss too the importance of predators in keeping deer populations healthy.

Touch Crawl

Touch Crawl focuses on increasing one's sensitivity to touch more than merely relying on audio clues to return to a point of origin. Blindfold all participants and spread them out at random in a forest (with little underbrush), a meadow, or an alpine tundra area.

Let all participants become familiar with the feel of the environment immediately surrounding the spot where they have been positioned.

A Taste Trail might involve gathering different types of tree pitch to compare their flavours.

The leader of the exercise should be moving about the area, speaking slowly but in a voice all can hear: "Think about the messages you are getting through your fingertips, not the name of the object you might be touching," the leader announces. "Now what are those message feelings? Are they soft? hard? rough? smooth? dry? wet? sticky? slimy? painful? pleasant? Think of the millions of messages your mind receives just through the sense of touch. Think too of all the creatures that rely on touch for most of their information.

"Let's become some of those creatures as we slowly work our way back to the spot where everyone was blindfolded. Imagine yourself as a snail. Crawl on your knees and elbows. Let your fingers be your antennae as you move slowly, ever so slowly [.011 kilometres per hour] across the landscape. Remember your sensors on the tips of your antennae; they can guide you safely on your journey. If something should startle you, curl up as if withdrawing inside your shell. When you come back out of the shell, do so slowly, cautiously. Feel for foods which might be edible, like nice succulent leaves. See if you can find a mate. Slowly, slowly ... ever so slowly."

If two or more participants by chance bump into one another, they

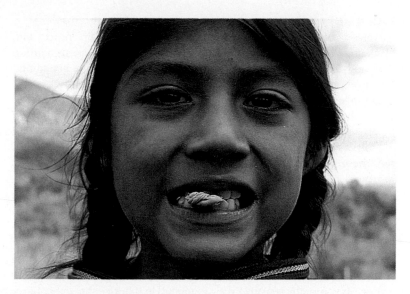

A Ute Indian boy displays the ponderosa pine pitch he has chewed into gum; the texture is perfect even if the taste is a bit unusual.

must identify each other through touch alone. No one speaks during this exercise except the instructor. Give the participants an opportunity to really tune in to becoming a snail before moving on to the next creature. If this exercise is too rushed, the messages are never brought home. Much of the effectiveness of this experience will depend on the mood set by the instructor and the persuasiveness of his or her voice.

"Let's explore this environment in yet another way," the instructor suggests to the creeping snails. "Without removing your blindfolds, let's become an animal that relies on smell more than vision to find its way. Let's all become moles or shrews. You have four legs now, so you'll be able to move much faster than a snail, but remember you're still very small — in fact, the world's smallest mammal. Crouch down low to the ground on your forearms and lower legs, and don't forget to sniff. What are those smell clues your mind is receiving? Are they sweet, pungent, musky? Can you smell something you might eat — a beetle, an earthworm? Remember now, you're still working your way back to the spot where you started." As each person ends up back at the spot where they started (or think they started), have them remove their blindfolds and be silently entertained by the shrews still returning to home base.

161

Taste Trail

"Have you ever wondered why a bird won't eat certain insects with black and yellow warning colourations?" a staff member asks as a group of youngsters are led along a nature trail. "Because it might get stung," a young girl suggests. "That's right," the instructor agrees, "but it also might mean the insect tastes awful. Have you ever noticed the way deer and rabbits taste their way along a trail — nibbling from plant to plant — obviously preferring some plants to others? Let's go on a taste trail ourselves. We won't use our hands now, only our lips and tongues. Let's see, these young fireweed shoots look good for a few nibbles." The instructor crouches down for a browse. "Ummm, not bad. Have a bite, then let's try these fresh spruce buds. Hmmm, a bit stringent, but quite edible. Anyone care for huckleberries? Nibble some leaves and then some berries right from the bush. Do they all taste the same to you?" the instructor asks. "The berries taste the same to me," answers a boy greedily extending his mouth for more. "Not to me," another child answers, "each one tastes a little different." "That's right," responds the leader. "If you really sensitize your tongue, you'll notice that every berry tastes slightly different from every other.

Taste Trail is an effective way to immerse youngsters in that often neglected fifth sense and to become more aware of the important role tasting plays in animal behaviour. It is also an absorbing way to learn more about edible wild plants. Warning: the instructor must be able to spot and avoid poisonous plants.

"Don't eat any mushrooms unless we can identify them," the instructor advises. "One of the shortcomings of our ability to taste is that poisonous things do not always taste bad. Now there's a fungus that's edible and easy to identify — notice the orange top and sulphur-yellow underside. See how it grows on trees instead of the ground. Nibble a bit and see if you can guess why it's called 'chicken of the woods.' "

Keep the group moving through a number of edible plants. If there is a safe drinking stream nearby, encourage everyone to take a drink by sipping from the surface rather than drawing the water up in their hands. "What does the water taste like? Sweet? Refreshing? Cold?" With refreshed taste buds, continue along the Taste Trail.

A nice addition to Taste Trail is to take some things back to camp to challenge everyone to a taste test. Have the group collect plants suitable for making teas: Labrador tea, licorice root, stinging nettle, chicory root, strawberry leaves, spruce buds, camomile, wild mint, edible berries, alder and sassafras bark. Back in camp, set some of each out on a table for all to see, smell, and touch. With the remaining part of each sample, make a tea. Pour a small taste for each participant and have them secretly record on an index card the name of the plant they think each tea was made from. After each taste test, have all participants hold up the guess written on their card, and keep score of correct responses. The winner of the taste test might just have sensitive enough taste buds to appreciate a taste treat — perhaps a fruit and nut candy bar.

CONNECTING

These activities are designed to help bring home one of the simplest, yet most frequently ignored, facts of life — everything is connected to everything else. When we admire a giant tree in the forest, how many of us draw the connection with the underground fungus and bacteria that is largely responsible for that tree's success? Water, phosphorus, and nitrogen would be largely unavailable to the tree without the mycorrhiza fungus that attaches to the tree roots and a nitrogen-fixing bacteria that lives with the fungus symbiotically. Without the tree and the flying squirrels that live in its branches, the fungus and bacteria could not reproduce effectively. Flying squirrels descend to the ground at night to dig up the fungus spore capsule for food. Every squirrel dropping becomes an "ecological pill" of live fungal spore, nitrogen-fixing bacteria, and the yeast nutrients necessary to propagate both throughout the forest.

Through the following activities youngsters not only learn to make connections between living things but, more important, to feel connected to all living things. Like the tree, fungus, bacteria, and squirrel interrelationship, they come to know the true meaning of interdependency — we can't make it alone.

Energy Pyramids

Pyramid models are one of the best ways to demonstrate how energy flows through a complex food web or a whole ecosystem. Energy Pyramids combines this lesson along with the fun and teamwork of building a human pyramid. A group of twelve or twenty participants is ideal, as it can be nicely divided into two three-tiered pyramids with six people per group, or two four-tiered pyramids with ten people per group. Extra players can act as team organizers.

To begin, the instructor should show participants a diagram of a food pyramid depicting the various trophic levels (levels of nourishment).

Green plants are on the bottom at trophic level one, because their energy has been transferred once from the sun to plants. Herbivores (plant eaters) are at trophic level two, because their energy has been transferred twice: from sun to plants and plants to herbivores. Carnivores (meat eaters) that eat herbivores are at trophic level three, because their energy has been transferred three times: from sun to plants, plants to herbivores, and herbivores to carnivores. High-level carnivores (those that eat other carnivores) are trophic level four because their energy has been transferred four times.

Once the participants understand the principle of energy transfer, the instructor should explain that this is a very simple model. "It is possible to have many more levels of a pyramid," the instructor points out. "For instance, it takes a lot of sunlight to grow single-celled sea plants, which provide food for microscopic sea animals, which feed needlefish, which in turn feed herring, which feed salmon, which ultimately feed a bear, eagle, killer whale, or human. We are going to look at three or four levels of that energy transfer in a pyramid-building contest."

Each team is now presented with a set of large index cards with animals or plants showing a particular energy flow printed boldly and illustrated on each. The object of the game is to see which team can build their pyramid and label each level first. Only correct labelling counts, so careful thought is as important to success as speed.

Some examples:

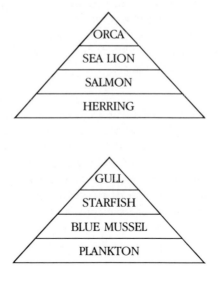

Energy Pyramids demonstrate how energy flows through a complex food web; it takes yet another form of energy to demonstrate it with kids.

The index cards can be strung to hang behind the neck of one player at each level, or, alternatively, they can simply be held in the mouth. The two teams build their pyramids directly facing one another so they are constantly aware of the other's progress as well as any errors in their logic.

The first team to have all their members in position with the correct labelling wins the set. Following the inevitable collapse of the pyramid, it is time to start over, with each team given a new set of cards. Five to six sets are usually sufficient to exhaust most everyone.

A short discussion should follow each pyramid-building session, to be certain all players understood why the energy transfer worked the way it did. An interesting addition to this game is to give four coloured tennis balls to the four bottom players in each pyramid. "These are pesticide balls," the instructor points out. "You must pass them up to each level above you, and the top-level predator must hold all four because that's where they end up in the real food pyramid. In a real world three-level food chain, the predator would get 111 "balls" because each lower trophic level is ten times larger than the one above."

Try another pyramid where the instructor says, "I wonder what would happen if we pulled out part of a level?" and proceeds to do so. "So what happens when the herring or shrimp get overfished? if oil spills kill the plankton? or too many high-level carnivores are exterminated?"

Be sure to choose a good location for this activity: sandy beach, soft grassy meadow, or mossy forest floor, and carefully monitor the event to prevent any injuries. Also be sure the smallest players end up on top.

Wanted Dead Or Alive

Wanted Dead or Alive is designed to follow Bigfoot. While the participants are busy compiling their surveys of the forest floor, the instructor stealthily hangs a sign from a nearby tree branch or bush. The sign reads: "Wanted Dead or Alive! Reward offered for information leading to the positive identification of a forest decomposer."

"What's a decomposer?" someone is sure to ask once the group discovers the sign. "That's a good question and an important one," the instructor answers. "Decomposers are animals and plants which help break down dead organic matter like leaves, needles, wood, and dead animals, and then convert them into chemicals that living plants and animals can use. Earthworms, termites, fly maggots, mites, beetles, mushrooms, and bacteria all aid in decomposition. They are all decomposers.

"Let's see how many decomposers each of you recorded on your Bigfoot list," the instructor suggests. "Use your pen to draw an arrow pointing up beside every living item on your list and one pointing down beside each dead item. Now draw an enclosing arrow beside each of the items you think might be a decomposer. Record your totals for Alive/Dead and Decomposers on the bottom of your sheet."

Example:

1) three types of moss
2) spruce pollen cone
3) hemlock cone
4) baby huckleberry
5) beetle
6) cedar twig

7) earthworm   ⚥ C
8) spider   ⚥
9) fern   ⚥
10) mould   ⚥ C
11) hemlock needle   ⚥
12) spruce-bud cap   ⚥
13) mushroom   ⚥ C
14) centipede   ⚥ C
15) deer dropping   ⚥
16) lichen   ⚥
17) alder leaf   ⚥
18) liverwort   ⚥
19) rotting wood   ⚥
20) baby hemlock tree   ⚥
21) soil bacteria   ⚥ C
22) roots   ⚥
23) termite   ⚥ C
24) spider-egg case   ⚥
Total Alive: sixteen
Total Dead: eight
Total Decomposers: seven

"What would happen if there weren't decomposers to break down the dead things that end up on the forest floor?" the instructor asks. Let each child express their view. "Decomposers are responsible for breaking down at least eighty percent of all plant material in the forest. We should never underestimate their role. The entire process of decomposition may take many years, especially in the case of fallen trees. Imagine if there were no decomposers: we would be surrounded by piles of natural litter, dead trees, and animals. The plants that make up the forest would be starved for nutrients and most would not survive. Dead or alive, Everything in this forest is important to the life cycle.

"Let's each find one dead thing here in the forest and give it a eulogy — describe one good deed it did during its life," the instructor now suggests. Each youngster gives their object a name and describes an important detail:

"This is Twiggy," a girl begins. "It supported some alder leaves during its life, and a bird might still use it for part of its nest."

"This is Bud" (a spruce-bud covering), a boy offers. "Bud protected the tip of a spruce branch during the frost. Bud was retired this spring."

"Dead or Alive, everything in nature is always Wanted."

"Connie the spruce cone provided a meal for a squirrel," another girl adds. "Had Connie not had her seeds eaten, she might have produced a lot of baby spruce."

"This dead insect doesn't really have a name, but it probably pollinated a lot of flowers during its life," suggests another.

"Nell, the hemlock needle, spent its entire life converting energy from the sun into food to nourish a tree," the last child contributes.

The instructor now asks everyone to set their object down on the ground "so the decomposers can get to work."

The instructor concludes: "Before we leave this spot, let's all find a seed [acorn, spruce-cone seed, or maple seed] to plant beside the object we each set down to decompose. Remember, the building materials of life must be used over and over again. Everything in nature is always wanted — dead or alive!"

Prey On Prey

An instructor leads a group of youngsters into a sphagnum bog, commenting: "I'll bet this place is teeming with life, even if it doesn't appear like much. Let's take a close look at this muskeg or bog community. There are a number of predator and prey species constantly interacting here in a life and death struggle." (Explain the words predator and prey, if necessary.) "For instance, dragonfly larvae prey on stickleback fish in the bog ponds, and both in turn are preyed on by cutthroat trout. Sundew plants trap and digest insects (such as mosquitoes), but they in turn may be grazed by deer. The mosquito preys on the deer but also provides food for the stickleback, the cutthroat, and the adult dragonfly. Red-throated loons eat both stickleback fish and cutthroat trout, but they in turn are eaten by peregrine falcons. Mosquitoes prey on both loons and falcons, and all these animals, when dead, become food for decomposers: worms, beetles, maggots, fungi, and bacteria. Wow, what a jungle!"

Throughout this discussion, the instructor holds up cards with illustrations (or photos) and the names of the various interacting species. These cards are laminated so they can withstand wetness and rough play.

"Now that we know how all these creatures interact, let's become some of them and see how we interact," the instructor challenges.

Seven participants might get the following labels safety-pinned to their backs: 1) dragonfly; 2) dragonfly larva; 3) stickleback fish; 4) cutthroat trout; 5) sundew plant; 6) deer; 7) mosquito. Each youngster can easily see what everyone else is, but must discover their own secret identity by asking questions which can be answered Yes or No. For example: Do I fly? Do I swim? Do I lay eggs? Do I release pollen and flower? Do I give live birth? Am I a bear? Am I a bird? The questions continue, everyone asking and answering at once until someone finds out what they are. While others are still trying to guess their identity, those who know are allowed to attack their prey. Prey on Prey involves chases, lunges, falls, and playful wrestling on the ground if the prey is mobile enough to escape. A deer nibbling on a sundew, of course, would be less active, but equally silly. Prey can be attacked before they know their identity, and everyone must come back to life after every capture so they can involve themselves in another predator/prey interaction.

Prey on Prey requires a cushioned terrain for falling and light wrestling: a sandy beach, bog, shallow pond, mossy forest, or grassy meadow. The species interaction one chooses to illustrate should be appropriate to each specific terrain.

When the roughhousing settles down, call all the players together to discuss how each fits into their community. How does each contribute? Who isn't important? Is one more important to the community than another? See how many can find the animal or plant they represent in the bog. Hand out paper and pencils and ask each youngster to compose a poem or a limerick about their creature and its role in the bog community. Example:

What a wonderful plant is the sundew
Its leaves are covered in sticky glue
Unlike most plants
This one eats ants
But sometimes a deer might chew a few.

Tide Pool Community

Tide Pool Community is a good follow-up activity to Octopus Garden (described earlier) where youngsters are still gathered around the tide pool each has been exploring. "Now that everyone's had a chance to see and feel their tide pool dwellers, let's look at how they interact."

The instructor briefly describes the role each tide pool dweller plays in their community: the primary food producers (eelgrass, kelp, corraline algae); the grazers (limpets, chitons, snails); the filter feeders (barnacles, mussels, plume worms); and the carnivores (anemones, hermit crabs, starfish, dog whelks, and sculpins).

The instructor hands out clipboards with paper and coloured felt pens. Each paper is labelled: "Octopus Garden — Tide Pool Community." On the bottom of the sheet is a place for one's name, while a large circle in the centre represents one's tide pool. "Find one animal or plant in your garden that you especially like and draw it somewhere in your circle," the instructor suggests. "Now find something else that your creature depends on and draw that with an arrow pointing from your first creature to the thing it depends on." This continues until the artists have linked a number of animals and plants in a community relationship. Compare examples between the participants before moving on to the last stage of the exercise.

"We've had a chance to see, feel, and explore the relationships between intertidal creatures — now let's become some of them," the instructor says. (A sandy or gravel beach works best for this stage of the exercise.)

Five volunteers are arranged on the beach like the five arms of a starfish. (Lying on bellies with hands clasped and heads touching, a human starfish is formed.) Challenge the starfish to co-ordinate its body

171

A "wolf" signals that he's found his territorial boundary in Wolf Pack Territory.

arms to move ten feet to one side, where a cluster of barnacles and mussels might make a nice meal. Anyone not already a part of the starfish can become mussels and barnacles by clustering tightly together in foetal positions. Let the starfish reach the other players before introducing the next creature. "Oh, oh," the instructor warns, "there's a crab looking for a meal too!" Three children become a crab, the one in the middle hugging the waist of the child on either side. (A squeeze of the waist activates one or both claws, the extended arms of the children on either side.) While the crab is milling about, practising its sideward walking and snapping its claws, yet another creature enters the stage. Starfish and mussel/barnacle players regroup to become an octopus. Eight children lock their left hands together to form the octopus head, while their right arms reach outward as the probing, tentacled arms of a large octopus. If the crab looks concerned at this new creature, it should be. "Octopus love to eat crabs," the instructor informs. "They ambush their victims, overwhelm them, and tear them apart with their powerful arms. An octopus can crack the shell of a crab with its powerful, parrot-like beak, located on the underside of the head. If I was a crab, I'd be looking for a place to hide right about now." Let the ensuing action play itself out while keeping an eye out for everyone's safety.

Wolf Pack Territory

Wolves maintain rigidly controlled territories by urinating at key scent markers on the perimeter of their range. As no two wolves have the same urine scent, these boundaries are easily distinguished. To simulate this situation for humans, bottled oils may be used. Garlic, lemon, and peppermint oils are easily distinguishable, and can be purchased in small, portable bottles from any spice section of a supermarket.

The instructor uses three different scented oils to secretly mark out the edges of the three make-believe wolf territories. Large rocks, fallen trees, open earth patches, or tree trunks all make for likely scent sites. When daubed with the scented oils, these markers take on a very realistic look indeed. Do not overlap the wolf territories when laying out the boundaries; ideally, all packs should be in distinct view of one another while playing the game. A total circumference of fifty metres is usually adequate for each pack's territory.

There should be only one or two scent markers for every participant playing the game, and none of the youngsters should have any idea that the area has been marked out beforehand.

Divide the players into three equal-sized packs, and scent the ankle of the largest boy in each group. Have the packs get familiar with their pack scent by sniffing the ankle of their alpha male. Some discussion of the wolf's highly organized social structure, centering on a dominant male and a dominant female, might be in order. "A dominant wolf holds its tail high, stands stiff-legged, and bristles its mane," the instructor comments. "In its presence, a subservient animal cowers on the ground with its ears back, or stands with its tail between its legs." Encourage the participants to act out their social positions, then kneel and rehearse howling as a pack so that each individual is familiar with the distinct call of their group. Wolf howling may be a "song fest" for sheer enjoyment or a way of warning other packs to keep away from occupied territory.

Give careful instructions to each pack to search out, by sniffing, the edge of their territory. When an individual wolf has located the correct scent, they are to kneel at that site and howl until all other members in their pack are doing the same. If an individual gets confused trying to locate their scent marker, they must search out their alpha male to get another sniff of his ankle.

When all players of a pack have located a scent marker and are kneeling and howling wildly, the alpha male will now be able to determine the centre of his territory. All wolves in the pack are to immediately join him there for a great community howl. The first pack howling loudly in unison from the exact centre of their range will be declared the dominant pack.

Big Bad Wolf

Big Bad Wolf acts as a natural extension to Wolf Pack Territory. Let the dominant pack continue to play the role of wolves while all other players become habitat: food, water, or territory. Have the two teams of players line up facing one another over an open running area, fifteen to twenty metres apart. The habitat players are each given a set of three 8-x-10 cards with drawings titled: 1) Territory (a forest and tundra); 2) Food (deer and caribou); and 3) Water (a lake and creek).

Each of these components of habitat are necessary for the wolves' survival. Both teams of players now turn their backs to one another. The habitat players choose one of their three cards to display in front of the other two, while the wolf players choose one of three postures to represent their greatest immediate need: 1) Territory (their arms are stretched out wide to their sides); 2) Food (both hands hold their bellies); and 3) Water (both hands cover the mouth). When the instructor gives the signal to turn around, the wolves immediately have to run toward that habitat element they are signalling that they most need. Every wolf successful in finding territory, food, or water lives to reproduce. Each habitat player a wolf has thus captured returns their habitat cards to the instructor and joins the wolf team. Any wolf unsuccessful in matching up their need with a habitat player, dies and becomes part of the habitat. The instructor then gives that player habitat cards.

The dynamics of this game are surprisingly similar to the interplay between any species and its habitat. As long as there is sufficient food, water, and territory, the species prospers. A reduction in the availability of any or all of the above results in population decline.

Play this game five to six times, so the participants can better understand the dynamics. Now introduce a new factor. Exchange a few of the Food (deer and caribou) cards with cards depicting sheep. Do this when the wolves have their backs turned, so they cannot anticipate this change. When the signal is given to turn around, some wolf is likely to attack a sheep. Ask that person (or persons) why they changed food sources. "Because it was there, or there wasn't anything else to eat" are exactly the reasons real wolves behave in the same way. "Well, there's a rancher in this area now," the instructor warns, "and you're a dead wolf. Any others I see killing sheep will also be shot." The two teams line up again, and this time all the Territory cards showing forest and tundra are replaced with cards depicting a new housing development. If the wolves appear puzzled when they rush for Territory, they should be. Families with small children won't move into a housing development where wolves prowl about. The developers must shoot or poison them. There shouldn't be many wolves left at this point, but any final players in search of water may discover a diversion project moving the creek through a pipeline to a distant city. The game is over.

"One hundred years ago wolves were more widely distributed than any other mammal of historic times," the instructor tells the subdued players. "Today their range is greatly reduced due to changes in habitat and human effort to exterminate them. In 1950 a hunter in British Columbia shot the last Cascade Mountain wolf in the world; he had wiped out an entire subspecies. The stereotype image of the big bad wolf has followed Europeans to this continent, and the extermination of the species there is being repeated on our shores.

"What does it mean to us that there are no more Cascade Mountain wolves?" asks the instructor. "It makes me sad," says one girl, "wolves are so beautiful." "Does that mean now that the Cascade Mountain wolf is gone forever, the world is a little less beautiful?" "I think so," says another girl. "So do I," agrees the boy who had been the last surviving wolf of the game. "There's another way to look at it," says the instructor. "Imagine that the world is like a car made up of animals and plants. Every single species of plant and animal has a special role to play to keep the world running. What happens if a lug nut falls off the wheel and disappears, like the Cascade Mountain wolf?" "The wheel is loose," suggests one girl. Another says, "The car can still run." The instructor adds, "But not as well as it used to, and what if it loses more parts? What then?

"There are many endangered species besides wolves," the instructor continues, "and we are losing them at alarming rates. Each of us are going to have to do something significant in our lifetimes to reverse that trend, or our grandchildren will inherit an earth impoverished in every way from the one we know now. What can we do?" Participants suggest solutions ranging from writing a letter to the newspaper to making posters that will teach people about a certain animal. Other good suggestions to mention are: learn as much as you can about plants and animals (read books and magazines and watch television shows about nature); don't buy or keep animals that have been taken from the wild; don't buy anything that has been made from the fur, skin, feathers, or other parts of endangered species; never kill any animal unnecessarily; and support groups that are working to save threatened animals. "Let's make a secret pledge here today on which action each of us will take to help preserve an endangered species." The instructor hands out paper, pens, and envelopes, then circulates a stamp pad. "Once you've made your pledge, swear to it by leaving your fingerprint as your signature. Use the stamp pad. Remember now, this is a promise to yourself. Your fingerprint, like every creature on this planet, is unique and special." The secret pledges can be sealed in each participant's envelope containing their Letters to the Future and drawings from their Spirit Spots.

Three's A Crowd

Three's A Crowd was inspired by a group of youngsters returning from an Eagle Eyes exercise on Haida Gwaii's Rediscovery. As they passed by the shore below an eagle nest, they were astonished to see a downy eaglet jump out of the nest. The bird landed unhurt in a patch of salal bush, but it had no way of returning to the nest. Because the bird

The last Cascade Mountain wolf sends out a song to the rest of its kind that is never answered.

took the daring leap before it even had feathers, the kids named it "Eagle Knievel." The kids made a nest for the eaglet on shore, and, remarkably, the parent eagles delivered food to the site. During the next few weeks, the young bird grew and became fully feathered, relying solely on wild foods brought by the parents.

Eagle Knievel was a lucky one. Normally a pair of eagles only fledge one or two young. Any bird unfortunate enough to fall from a nest almost certainly will perish from hunger, cold, or predators.

Three's A Crowd teaches the law of survival; it works well as a continuation of the Eagle Eyes exercise described in Sensing. Two participants are chosen for the role of parent eagles.

"See how many eaglets you've hatched out here?" the instructor points out to the parent eagles. "Now you must try to provide for all of them. Let's pretend the small cookies in this bag represent eagle food you've captured in the surrounding area. There can be no human talking now, just eagle calls and the cry of hungry eaglets." Everyone practises their calls and positions. Those youngsters delegated to the role of baby eaglets must kneel upright with hands clasped behind their backs, and mouths wide open awaiting cookies. The parent eagles practise their feeding technique, each using their hand as a simulated beak for dropping a cookie into the waiting mouths.

"Of course, both parents rarely return to the nest with food at the same time," the instructor points out. "So let's see what happens when only one cookie at a time is brought to the hungry young."

The two parent eagles now take turns alternately delivering one cookie and then turning their backs and covering their eyes (to simulate flying out of sight) while the second parent delivers a cookie to the greedy mouths. There should be two types of cookies in the bag, very different in colour and flavour (ginger snaps and vanilla wafers work well). After eight to twelve cookies have been delivered to the nest, ask the eaglets which one of them received the most. Invariably, one or two will have received far more than their fair share, while some will have gone hungry. As in the real world of eaglets, those improperly nour-ished do not survive. Survivors are normally the first eagle chicks to hatch, for these are always somewhat larger and stronger than the youngest. Now that the survivors have been determined, ask them if they happened to consume any of the ginger snaps. "That's too bad," the instructor says in a sad voice. "That particular food contains very high levels of pesticide. Even a well-fed eagle with too high a pesticide level will not be successful in reproducing as an adult if the poisoning persists."

Before ending Eagle Eyes, discuss with the group how man-made toxins enter the food chain of high-level predators and affect survival and reproduction. Suggest things we can do to alleviate this threat to these magnificent birds (such as eliminating the use of DDT and restricting the use of other pesticides), then share the leftover cookies with the parents and still-hungry eaglets.

Hungry, Hungry Marten

In a forest setting, ask the group to name as many animals as they can that live in the temperate forests: bear, deer, raccoon, squirrel, toads, woodpeckers, thrushes, mice, shrew, weasel, and marten. Discuss how the forest provides food and shelter for these species, and the range of territory each might hold within the forest. For instance, the home range of the marten is largely determined by food availability. A few square kilometres may be sufficient in times of abundance, but up to thirty-eight square kilometres will be required in times of scarcity. Red squirrels are an important part of a marten's diet, but their home range is much smaller. A marten can do everything a squirrel can do — climb trees, and leap from branch to branch with great speed and agility.

The advantage the squirrel has in escaping the marten is that it knows its home range better. Squirrels have highways in the treetops and on the ground that they know by heart; they also have refuge holes inside trees too small for the marten to enter.

Choose one volunteer to be a marten. (Two marten should be chosen if the group is large — more than six to nine.) All other players become squirrels. The squirrels have one tree in the forest that provides marten-proof shelter. If they can reach this tree and shout "Hungry, Hungry Marten" before a marten tags them, then they are home free. The game begins with the squirrels out gathering cones some distance away from their refuge tree. Suddenly, the instructor shouts: "There's a marten on the hunt!" All squirrels scatter. The marten can position itself near this refuge during the game, but unless it pursues some squirrels for a meal it will surely go hungry. The squirrel family will discover that the best strategy for getting home free is to combine a lot of squirrel chatter with a lot of fast movement to distract and confuse the marten.

The game can actually be played two ways. The object of one version is to get as many squirrels as possible (preferably all) to the home tree. In a second version, even faster paced, each time a squirrel safely reaches the tree and shouts "Hungry, Hungry Marten," he or she

Haida Gwaii Rediscovery kids dubbed this eaglet Eagle Knievel when it jumped from its nest before it was fledged. Three's A Crowd teaches the laws of natural selection.

immediately becomes the new marten and the former marten becomes a squirrel.

Speed, agility, camouflage, and surprise are all key elements in the strategies of both squirrel and marten. Expect to be winded after this game. While everyone catches their breath, the instructor should point out that only a century ago the marten was quite common throughout the extensive forests of North America. He or she asks, "How many of you have seen a marten?" Most likely no one in the group has ever spotted a marten.

Today the species is one of the rarest predators in North America because so much of its forest habitat has been lost. In the past few decades, one-half of all the old-growth forests on the planet have been cut. "What does that mean to animals like the marten and countless others?" the instructor asks. "In saving parks and wild areas, how much is enough? Would a twenty-square-kilometre forest preserve protect squirrels? Would it protect marten? Remember, if one marten, in times of scarcity, requires up to thirty-eight square kilometres, and it takes two marten to reproduce, then we need a much larger area. An even larger area will be required to protect a healthy population. Maintaining the biological diversity, the great complexity of animals and plants, of this planet will be one of the greatest challenges your generation will face."

Time Travellers

It is difficult for almost everybody to comprehend the incredible age of the earth (an estimated 4.6 billion years) and the sequence of events that lead up to our moment in earth's lifetime. Time Travellers puts youngsters on a hiking journey through time, helping them to understand earth history by relating distances on a hike with significant chronological earth events.

"Imagine what it would be like if we could actually go back in time and experience the events which shaped the earth," a hike leader says, as a group of children are tightening the straps on their backpacks; "Well, that's exactly what we're about to do." "You mean we might see dinosaurs?" an inquiring child interrupts. "Not exactly," the leader responds, "but I'll bet we see some of the species of plants and insects which lived in the age of the dinosaurs. Now let's not forget to take our passports. This is a very long journey."

Handmade passports labelled: *Time Traveller Passport* are handed out to each person in the group. There is space on the first page for name, date of birth, and place of birth. Sixteen blank pages provide space for stamps, stickers, or drawings to illustrate significant moments in earth time. The top of each page has two lines labelled *Dateline* and *Event* which the Time Travellers will fill in as they go. The bottom of the passport has a continuous line running from page one and dated "4.6 billion years," to the end of page sixteen dated "present."

At the end of the passport are four blank pages for drawings and thoughts about earth creation theories that are different from the one that will be presented on the hike. Along the way, hikers should be reminded that the idea that the earth is 4.6 billion years old is only one theory, and that scientists are always discovering new clues to the earth's beginning and changing their own theories. Emphasize that there is no one right way to think about earth creation, and that all beliefs have validity.

Time Travellers can be a day exercise set out over a course one or two kilometres long, but it is especially effective when conducted over a three or four day, twenty kilometre (or more) backpack expedition. For most youngsters, this will be the farthest they have ever hiked in their lives, so the distance profoundly influences their understanding of earth time. Along the hike route, sixteen signposts marking earth history events are set out by a staff member moments before hikers reach each distance. Here, passports must be presented for stamping. Each signpost is positioned at a specific distance and each has a large laminated index card suspended from it by a string. One side of the card has an illustration of the time period (example: dinosaurs, tree ferns, huge dragonflies) and a dateline. The reverse side has a description of the events of the time period and a few questions to stimulate discussion. The following example is modelled on a twenty-kilometre hike.

0 km.: 4.6 billion years ago: *The Solar System and Earth Forms*

A swirling disc-like cloud of gas and dust condenses to form our solar system, which includes the sun, planets, moons, asteroids, meteorites, dust, gas, and earth itself. Questions: Can anyone still see evidence of this event? Where?

.5 km.: 4.5 billion years ago: *Earth, an Alien Planet*

Earth is a very different planet from the one we know today. It's large and gaseous, close in size to Saturn, with an atmosphere of cosmic gases and a rocky, molten core. A huge output of heat from the sun strips away this first atmosphere. Question: If life had evolved on this gaseous planet what might it have been like?

5 km.: 3.75 billion years ago: *A New Atmosphere for Earth*

A new atmosphere forms around the earth as its molten surface begins to cool. The earth's crust solidifies, giving off gases which include water vapour, carbon dioxide, and nitrogen. The gases are like the fumes from volcanoes and hot springs. The water vapour in the gases condenses and falls back to earth as rain, starting the formation of lakes and oceans. Questions: How do the water and air cycles work? Could there be life without these cycles?

9.5 km.: 2.5 billion years ago: *Earth, A Lonely Planet*

For over half its existence the earth is devoid of life. Even after the formation of a solid crust and true oceans, its intense volcanic activity adds gases and water vapour to the atmosphere. These gases contain little oxygen and only tiny, jellyfish-like cells form in the oceans.

12 km.: 1.9 billion years ago: *Life Creates Life*

Different forms of algae and plant life evolve in the oceans, producing and releasing large amounts of oxygen into the atmosphere. This process of producing oxygen from carbon dioxide is called photosynthesis. Questions: Are plants necessary for the survival of animals on this planet? What happens when we cut down the forests?

15.5 km.: 1 billion years ago: *The Ozone Layer Appears*

Primitive algae have now produced enough oxygen to develop an ozone layer around the earth shielding the planet from the most damaging of the sun's rays and allowing for the evolution of more complex plants and animals. Question: What is the danger of ozone depletion today through human activity, i.e., burning fossil fuels, and releasing pollutants into the atmosphere?

17 km.: 600 million years ago : *First Animals Appear*

The first invertebrates (animals without backbones) evolve in the oceans: worms, trilobites, clams, barnacles, corals, and starfish are among the earliest animals on earth. Question: Why didn't animals evolve before plants?

18.5 km.: 290 million years ago: *Land Animals Appear*

All life on earth evolves through natural selection to occupy new environments. Life is found in great variety in the air, in fresh water, in the sea, and on land. As soon as the land is habitable, it is invaded by many different living things. First come plants. Giant ferns, horsetails, and club mosses grow in the burgeoning forests. Insects, scorpions, and giant spiders appear. Some dragonflies were seventy-five centimetres long (longer than your arm). Some fish evolve legs to replace their fins, and lungs to replace their gills, becoming the first amphibians. Questions: What does survival of the fittest mean? Have any types of plants or animals survived from this era?

18.75 km.: 220 million years ago: *Reptiles Appear*

Some amphibians are able to lay eggs which can develop on land. These animals have no need to return to the sea, some develop into early reptiles which give rise to early mammals. The reptiles evolve, to fill most of the ecological niches with everything from small chicken-like creatures to immense plant-eaters and horrific meat-eaters. (We call these reptiles dinosaurs.) They flourish on the earth, while mammals remain small, never getting much bigger than large rats. Questions: Why might the dinosaurs have become so huge while the mammals remained small? What happened to the mammals after the dinosaurs died off?

19 km.: 180 million years ago: *Birds Fly High*
Birds are direct descendants of the Ornithischia order of dinosaurs. (The feathers we see on birds today, according to theory, are just complex and highly evolved scales.) The first birds are dinosaurs with feathers, and they can't fly. They make long swooping jumps from low trees onto unsuspecting prey. Questions: How do birds differ from mammals? Are all the dinosaurs really extinct?

19.5 km.: 100 million years ago: *The Continents Separate*
The continents are like huge drifting rafts that float around the earth at the rate of one or two centimetres a year. The positions of land and sea are always changing. A single huge continent slowly starts to separate along fault lines and the smaller land masses begin to drift toward the positions they are today. Question: How did the separation of the continents affect plants and animals?

19.65 km: 64 million years ago: *Extinction of the Dinosaurs*
Nobody is exactly sure what caused the extinction of most dinosaurs. Their demise is followed by the evolution of huge flightless, meat-eating birds. Mammals grow into a group as varied and successful as the dinosaurs had been. One of these mammals is the primitive hedgehog that feeds at night on snakes and spiders. The largest animals in the forest are crocodiles and alligators.

15 metres before the end of the hike: 3.6 million years ago: *Our Ancestors Appear*
Ape-like people, capable of walking upright and using stone tools, now populate part of East Africa. Question: What advantage could be gained from an upright stance and the use of tools?

6 cm. before the end of the hike: 12,000 years ago: *Indians Arrive*
Undisputed evidence proves humans present in the Americas. Questions: What changes came with the arrival of humans? Did hunting by the newcomers have any effect on wildlife? Do you believe that native people first arrived via a Siberian land bridge during the last ice age, or do you think they arrived in a different way, at a different time?

2 mm. before the end of the hike: 500 years ago: *Immigrants Arrive*
People from all over the world establish permanent settlements in the

Time Travellers on Haida Gwaii Rediscovery explore ammonites and scallop fossils in shale.

Americas. Questions: What are some of the changes in the Americas in the past five hundred years? How have the plants and animals been affected?

End of hike: 75 years ago: *The Average Lifetime*
Your life is represented by one grain of sand on your fingertip compared to the twenty kilometres you have just hiked. Question: What changes will occur on earth in the infinitesimally short span of your life? How will a doubling of the world's human population affect the other creatures on earth?

Obviously, at the end of this hike many signposts are crowded very closely together. The situation would be even more difficult to portray accurately on a one-kilometre hike. Throughout the experience, hike leaders should try to point out natural history features which correspond to the time period the group is hiking through. For instance: outcrops of bedrock formed millions of years ago, fossils, glacial deposits, tide pool life, early plants like algae, ferns, horsetails, early insects like dragonflies, birds and mammals, at the appropriate time.

185

Encourage the youngsters to records their impressions as Time Travellers in their hike journals. Sylvan Dangert, an eleven-year-old Time Traveller on Haida Gwaii's Rediscovery, wrote:

In the sea of life
we are a grain of sand,
a speck of dust in this great land.
Eagle eyes and raven's wings
are the great things.
Meadows and trees tall,
those are best of all.
The unscratched surfaces are beautiful,
but the scratched rock is nice
like sheep's wool.
In nature we are listener,
and speaker as well;
measure your doings
as well.

Now it's time for them to find a quiet spot alone for fifteen or twenty minutes to fill in the last pages in their passport. Before they do this, the leader could briefly tell them other creation myths. Don't rush this. Let individuals take as much time as they need to write or draw about their feelings and ideas, about how the earth began and their place in it. If they aren't sure what they believe, then they can include some of the different ideas that they know about.

Hold a little ceremony as all the Time Travellers enter the last stamps in their passport. Remind them that although their lives may appear insignificant in earth time, they are going to have to do some significant things in that time to protect the environment, so that the legacy of life continues.

Beach-Life Bingo

Beach-Life Bingo was developed on Haida Gwaii's Rediscovery to help reinforce lessons in marine biology and food gathering. It also serves as a great indoor activity on a stormy day. The bingo cards are larger than normal and have coloured pictures of marine life in each of the squares usually reserved for numbers. The names and pictures of all these marine creatures are printed on cards and drawn randomly from a barrel, just as in regular bingo. Of course, no two playing cards are identical, so the same elements of chance and luck prevail.

Time Travellers walk through 4.5 billion years of earth history.

If the caller should pull the card for Pisaster starfish, the players now have to distinguish between several other species of starfish: bat stars, sunflower stars, and blood stars. If the group has too much trouble with this, the caller can show the picture on the name card. Clamshells are used in place of bingo chips. To expand the learning potential of the game, the participants set clamshells face down on those marine creatures living primarily on sand or sand/mud beaches, and face up if they are found on solid-rock habitat.

Of course, this concept can be applied equally well to any ecosystem with its community of plants and animals. Use pine-cone bingo chips in Forest-Life Bingo, or stones for Desert-Life Bingo.

Standard variations on the game can be used to determine winners: one line in any direction, a cross, vertical, horizontal, or blackout bingo, where all squares must be covered. Prizes can range from sweets to a certificate good for a free turn off dish-washing duty.

Crazy Fate

Crazy Fate is a card game, not unlike Crazy Eights, except that a normal card deck is replaced with the names (or pictures) of living things. All players are dealt eight cards, with the remainder stacked face down in the centre of the table. The top card is turned upright beside the main deck. The dealer plays on it or passes and picks up a new card.

Each person plays in turn, clockwise, starting with the dealer. Cards that show something that preys or is preyed upon by the existing face-up card are played face up on top of it. For instance, for a rabbit face-up card, any plant which rabbits eat (their "prey") or any rabbit predator (fox, wolf, coyote, etc.), including decomposers that "eat" dead rabbits, such as bacteria or maggots can be played. If the player does not have a card that plays he or she draws a card from the deck and passes.

If the player has mouse, bacteria, grass, fox, starfish, spruce tree, squirrel, and grasshopper cards when the face up card is a rabbit, play could go as follows: rabbit eaten by fox, fox eats mouse, mouse eats grasshopper, grasshopper eats grass, dead grass is consumed by bacteria, bacteria consumes dead squirrel, squirrel eats spruce tree cones. If the player decides to claim that the spruce tree is consumed by a starfish, the other players could challenge shouting "Crazy Fate." That player would then have to pick up all cards played on the rabbit card and draw a card from the deck and lose the turn.

The object of this game is to get rid of all your cards. A staff member may have to be called upon at times to verify a claim. Can an amoeba

Beach-Life Bingo (top) uses clamshells for bingo chips in reinforcing lessons in marine life on Haida Gwaii, while Rediscovery Four Corners uses piñon pine cones (below) to cover plants and animals of the desert.

eat a sea urchin? No, crazy fate.

Mystery Guess

Youngsters love the fun of guessing games, and this one has become an all-time favourite at several Rediscovery camps.

Mystery Guess introduces campers to animal characteristics and behaviour traits in a memorable and activity-oriented way. The object of the game is to guess the animal to which the staff give clues at every group meal. For instance, at breakfast the mystery clue read out to the group and posted on the dining-hall wall might be: "I have 27,000 teeth on my tongue and I rasp my food." Small pieces of paper, pens, and a ballot box are all located nearby for the participants to secretly record their guesses. All guesses will be read out loud at the next meal, and if no one gets the correct answer a new clue for the same mystery guest is posted: "I can stretch several times my normal length." Again, if no one guesses correctly, the dinner clue might be: "It takes me about 100 hours to travel a kilometre."

The clues get progressively easier until someone guesses correctly: "I am strictly a vegetarian."

"Gardeners find me a nuisance."

"I no longer have a shell like my near cousins." It may take a few days to get a correct answer, but eventually someone will guess a slug. There is no point in sharing a hunch with others in the group, as only the first correct answer pulled from the ballot box wins. Prizes can range from an extra dessert serving to that most coveted of prizes: a certificate good for one free turn off the chore of one's choice. With no shortage of incentive here on the part of the participants, the camp staff needs to be as creative and informative as possible in providing the clues to animals and plants found in the bioregion of the camp. A few examples from Haida Gwaii's Rediscovery:

Clues:

1. I can fit through an opening the size of my mouth or larger.
2. I always return to my home to eat.
3. I am very shy, and hunt mostly at night.
4. I always clean up my home after every meal.
5. I express my emotions by changing colours, and am regarded as quite intelligent.
6. I crack open crabs, cockles, and clams with my beak.
7. I have more arms than three humans combined.

Answer: Octopus

Clues:
1. There are more than a thousand different species of me.
2. I am found on every continent.
3. When I wake up in the morning, I stretch, I yawn, and I wash myself just like humans.
4. Some of my kind milk aphids like cows, others grow fungus on leaf cuttings for food.
5. I am incredibly strong and can carry an object ten times my body weight.
6. I leave a scent trail for others of my kind to follow.
Answer: Ant

Clues:
1. The male of my species is extremely territorial.
2. I am never found far from water.
3. My ancestors were much bigger in the time of the dinosaurs.
4. I prey on stickleback fish, but only as a juvenile.
5. Most of my life is lived underwater.
6. Females of my species oviposit eggs on the surface of fresh water.
7. I can hover in flight like a hummingbird.
Answer: Dragonfly

Clues:
1. I can accelerate fifty time faster than the space shuttle.
2. I can survive months without feeding.
3. I have claimed more human victims than all the wars ever fought.
4. I can jump one hundred and fifty times my own length — vertically or horizontally — equivalent to a person jumping nearly three hundred metres.
5. I can withstand enormous pressure, and remain frozen for a year then revive.
Answer: Flea

Clues:
1. I live high up in trees, on tree trunks, and on barren rock and tundra.
2. I absorb my food directly from the air.
3. I am slow-growing, and one of the oldest living things on earth.
4. I am not one, but a partnership between two living things (alga and fungus).
5. I colonize bare rock and provide a foothold for green plants.

"I leave my footprints at night," might be a Mystery Guess clue for coyotes that roam the dunes adjacent to the Rediscovery Four Corners camp.

192

6. I am the favourite food of caribou.
Answer: Lichen

Eagles And Ravens

A fast-action contest between two teams, Eagles and Ravens, demands speed and agility on one hand, with quick thinking and intelligence on the other. It's a great physical workout, popular with the participants, and ideal for releasing any pent-up energy before an evening campfire. Divide the group into equal-size teams, distinguished with different-coloured kerchiefs tied around arms or used as headbands. The Eagle and Raven teams then assemble in two straight lines facing one another, about three to four metres apart. Each team has a "home free" end zone clearly marked out on the playing field, about twenty to thirty metres behind where they begin. The set-up resembles a small football field, with two end zones and the opposing teams facing each other on opposite sides of the fifty-yard line.

A staff member has prepared a list of twenty to thirty true-and-false statements, which will now be presented to the group. If the answer to the statement is true, the Eagles chase the Ravens. If the answer to the statement is false, the Ravens chase the Eagles. For every member of the opposing team that is tagged before they reach their end zone, a point is scored for the offensive team. Staff members at each end zone can act as referees to help record tags. Present an equal number of true and false statements to the teams. Sometimes a player shouts out the wrong answer and everyone reacts in error. The instructor can then shout out the correct answer and watch the fun as the pursuers suddenly become the pursued.

This is an ideal way to "test" the participants on the natural history or cultural knowledge they have learned. For instance, natural-history statements might be:

1. Spruce trees are more salt-tolerant than hemlock trees. True. (That is why more spruce grows along exposed coasts than hemlock.)

2. Bears have eyesight as good as eagles. False. (Bears are notoriously near-sighted while eagles have vision ten times better than our own.)

3. Sundews are plants which eat insects. True. (These insectiverous plants digest flies attracted to their sticky leaves.)

Cultural statements should be based on the indigenous culture in the area. For instance, on Haida Gwaii's Rediscovery, Haida culture would be the focal point.

4. Haidas have never had women chiefs. False. (There was a well-

known woman chief of Kiusta.)

5. Haida dugout canoes were carved from the Sitka spruce trees. False. (Western red cedar was always used because of its ease of carving, pliability, and natural oils which prevent rot.)

Common-sense statements are always good for laughs.

6. The sun always sets in the east. False. (It always sets in the west, and depending on the time of year and one's location, it can range from northwest to southwest.)

7. True north and magnetic north are often different directions. True. (How much difference depends on where on the earth you are.)

Statements which require everyone to look first before reacting, and to which the answer could be true or false depending on the moment, are perhaps the most fun.

8. The sky is partly cloudy.

9. Everyone playing this game is wearing runners.

10. The tide is now high.

11. It's raining.

At the completion of the game the final scores are tallied and the winner declared. Ties do occur, but even a team that wins by a large margin should be encouraged to share any prizes (cookies, cake, apples, et cetera) with their distinguished opponents.

COMMUNICATION

Animal communication covers an enormous spectrum, from the territorial song of a bird to the complex sonar signals of whales sent out along deep-sea thermal boundaries to others of their kind thousands of miles apart. Movement and body language are other important forms of communicating. The Northern dipper's exaggerated bobbing movements may help it communicate better with its mate (in its roaring rapids habitat) than would a bird call; and, of course, the erect tail and stiff gait of an alpha male wolf sends such a clear message of dominance to other wolves that growls are rarely called for.

To impart, to transmit, to make known, to succeed in conveying information is the real purpose of communicating, and these activities do just that. They do not stop with our finned, feathered, and furred friends, but extend into our own social dealings and distinctly human ways of getting our message across.

Wolf Howl/Bear Growl

Many animals use characteristic sounds or movements to communi-

"Whale!" "Shrimp." "Whale!" "Shrimp." Participants call out from within their small ocean circle during an Echo Location game.

cate with members of their own species, sometimes over great distances. The larger the group, the more fun and complex Wolf Howl/Bear Growl becomes. Gather everyone in a circle and count them off while handing out blindfolds: one, two, three, four, five, six .... Repeat the count from one to six until everyone has been assigned a number. "All ones are wolves," the instructor announces, "let's hear you howl. All twos are bears, let's hear you growl." Threes become hooting owls, fours crying loons, fives honking geese, and sixes bellowing moose. (Any other loud-calling animal can be used in this game, though it's best to choose animals from the local area.) If the group is less than rambunctious, the instructor may choose to demonstrate each call for them.

Once everyone has rehearsed their call, have them all blindfolded and set off in search of their own kind. This is not as easy a task as it might first appear, especially if all the animals are calling loudly and at once. The first species to successfully gather together all its members will be declared the winners.

Gathering everyone back in a circle and removing blindfolds, the instructor can now change the emphasis from sound to movement and body characteristics for interspecies identification. Bring into play the

195

less vocal species: rabbits, snakes, deer, ants, butterflies, or humming-birds. This time the instructor shows each player a card with the name of a silent animal listed on it. Each animal is shown only twice, so that everyone will be required to find one other of their kind. (If you have an odd number of players, show one card three times.)

"Does everyone know what they are?" the instructor asks. "Good! Now remember you must find your mate using body language only." Silent bedlam ensues.

Echo Location

Echo location is one of the communication marvels of the animal world, and nowhere is it better developed than in whales and dolphins. "Just think," an instructor says to a group of youngsters eager to play, "whales can actually 'see' with their ears. Have you ever opened your eyes underwater and discovered how short the distance is you can actually see? Even in clear, shallow water you can't see much farther than sixty metres and at depths of only four hundred metres the ocean is pitch black. But water carries sound farther and faster than it carries light. Some whales take advantage of this: they have evolved a process called echo location to 'see' with sound. Sperm whales can find giant squid in total darkness 3.2 kilometres below the surface using echo location. Blue whales can locate huge schools of shrimp and krill the same way.

"The way it works is pretty neat," the instructor says enthusiastically.

"To see what lies ahead in the dark ocean, a whale or dolphin sends out a sharp clicking sound. When the click reaches a school of fish or shrimp, it bounces back, like a ball bouncing off a wall. If the click returns quickly to the whale, it knows that the food is close. Besides locating food in this way, whales can also find directions and communi-cate with one another over incredible distances. Fin whales can send out sounds that can be heard 3,220 kilometres away!

"Who wants to be a blue whale hunting for shrimp in the total dark?" the instructor asks. An eager volunteer is blindfolded. Two or three others are chosen to be the shrimp. All other participants form a big ocean by joining hands in a circle. "Okay now," the instructor continues, "every time the whale shouts out in a deep voice 'Whale!', the shrimp must immediately respond in a high-pitched voice: 'Shrimp.' If the whale should shout 'Whale! Whale! Whale!', the shrimp must mimic with the sonar echo, 'Shrimp, Shrimp, Shrimp.' "

The whale must capture at least two shrimp, and be holding them

Porpoise, like whales and dolphins, use echo location to find their prey.

simultaneously, before he or she can be relieved of their whale duties. The first shrimp caught tends to get dragged around a bit before a second is captured, so the instructor must watch the situation carefully and be ready to step in if it gets too rough. The circle of players defining the boundaries of the game are not idle spectators in this drama. They can decide to put added pressure on the shrimp by closing the circle tighter and thus making the ocean smaller. This becomes necessary when a slow whale has difficulty capturing prey.

Any number of variations to this game are possible, such as sperm whale/squid, killer whale/salmon, porpoise/fish, and bat/bugs. It is easier for smaller players to be the predator, if they are only required to capture one prey.

Play this game several times, letting different players take on the predator/prey roles.

Talk Of The Town

Communication is not restricted to our furred, feathered, and finned friends. With unprecedented human demands on the earth's natural resources, it is not surprising that conflicts over land use increasingly dominate the Talk of the Town. Complex issues are often presented as black and white, win-lose situations, with rigid stereotypes depicting the players. Veterans of such conflicts can more fully appreciate the human factors that come into play in resolving these problems.

Talk of the Town, especially suited to youth in their late teens or Adult Rediscovery Sessions, can take place in a classroom or a wilderness camp where the area of conflict is intensified by the intimacy of natural surroundings. The activity casts players in typical resource-conflict roles but challenges them to re-evaluate stereotypes.

Begin the exercise by having all participants randomly select a role from a box of folded papers. Twelve typical roles might be: 1) public-relations officer for a hydro company; 2) fish and wildlife (game) officer; 3) senator or member of parliament for area; 4) president of local Chamber of Commerce; 5) Native Indian tribal leader; 6) editor of regional newspaper; 7) logging-company executive; 8) nuclear-power proponent; 9) national-news broadcaster; 10) mayor of city; 11) concerned citizen; and 12) director of large environmental group.

On the back of each role title, the position is briefly outlined. Examples:

Concerned Citizen: You are a fourth-generation resident of a community that will be flooded if the proposed hydro dam is built. You see the

198

need for more employment in the area, but your great-grandfather, Richard Hazameen, founded this town.

Mayor of City: Seacouver desperately needs a new source of power to supply the city's burgeoning population. The emissions from the old coal-burning generators has citizens up in arms, and it threatens to become an election issue.

Logging-Company Executive: There's big profits to be realized from clear-cutting the valley to be flooded, but who compensates your company for lost revenues from future forests in this part of your timber-licence area?

Native Indian Tribal Leader: Your people have occupied the Hazameen Valley for more than eight thousand years. Treaties dating from the 1800s protect your land "for as long as the river shall flow."

Once all the players know their identity and general positions, they draw at random from another box, marked Personality Trait. These might include:

1. You are very open and receptive to other people's comments.
2. You are uncompromising in your position and insist that others see things your way.
3. You are sexist and somewhat racist in your attitudes.
4. You are shy and experience great difficulty speaking in public.
5. You are easily persuaded to other viewpoints and tend to share the views of the person who most recently lobbied you.
6. You like to make personal attacks and accusations against people who differ from your position.

Once all participants are familiar with their roles and personality traits, the instructor presents a map outlining the conflict. The example illustrated here shows a proposed hydro dam capable of supplying the city of Seacouver (population 1 million) with all its energy needs until the year 2050. The proposal would reduce Seacouver's dependency on coal-burning generators (producing smog and acid rain), and would allow for the sale of additional power during peak flows to Vanatlle, across the international border. The difficulty with the plan is that it floods a prime wilderness recreation valley, destroys salmon and migratory corridors for endangered wildlife, floods part of an Indian reserve (a treaty violation), and requires the relocation of Hazameen (population 1,300). Whiskey Junction, currently little more than a bar and truck stop by the highway, would become the construction centre, swelling the population from 102 to 12,000 during peak construction. Nuclear-power proponents see alternatives for the power requirement

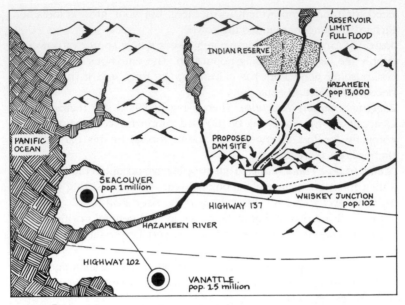

The hydroelectric dam proposed for the Hazameen Valley has become the Talk of the Town in this role-play exercise.

located much closer to Seacouver, but local citizens fear the potential for accidents.

This scenario can be greatly elaborated upon, and will be, as each player is called up to the map to outline their position before a commission. Staff or other camp participants can sit on the Commission, whose mandate is to review fairly all aspects of the proposal and make a recommendation to government.

Once all the preliminary submissions have been presented and the "media" have had an opportunity to question the participants, everyone will be required to draw from yet another situation box. This time the draw is for Change in Life. (While the following examples are extreme, it is not uncommon for similar situations to affect individuals in these circumstances.)

Examples:

1. Your doctor informed you this morning that you may have less than six months to live.
2. Your investments have been scrutinized and the media are about to publish a story suggesting conflict of interest in this issue.

3. Your spouse just won a million-dollar lottery, and you couldn't care less about your job.
4. You are secretly having an affair with one of the commissioners.
5. There has been a death in your family and you are extremely depressed.
6. A national magazine wants to feature you on their cover for the courageous stand you've taken on this issue.
7. Your spouse has just left you because you seem to care more about this commission than your family.

Because dinners and cocktail parties are as important in a lobby effort as the more formal forum, let the role-play continue during a lunch or dinner break. At the close of the informal session, reconvene the hearings, allowing each player to address the commission one final time.

Talk of the Town is an involved exercise, ideal for a rainy day in camp. It can actually be carried over from one day to the next if those involved become adequately absorbed. The commission's recommendations to government should also be commented upon by all the players. The resource issue may or may not be adequately resolved, but all parties will hopefully come away with better skills and understanding for addressing such challenges in the real world.

SURVIVING

These skills and activities open a different path of discovery and appreciation for the earth; they show how our living is connected to it and uses its store of resources. With a few simple survival skills learned at camp and an understanding of earth survival philosophy, youngsters can extend experiences of the natural world throughout their lives. Rocks take on a whole new dimension for the child who can spark fire from them, shape them into a tool, or arrange them into a trap or deadfall to procure small game. Trees become more than scenes in an abstract landscape when one knows how to fashion slingshots, bow-drills, and bows and arrows from their branches; cooking baskets, rope, and clothing from their bark and roots; fire starter, cut ointment, and chewing gum from their pitch — all without ever seriously hurting the tree. Knowing how to fill one's belly from nature's bounty of edible leaves, nuts, fruits, roots, insects, birds, fish, and mammals brings with it a satisfaction and sense of security no formal schooling can match.

Through such experiences, a person's need for the earth and use of its gifts becomes more real. Direct connections with nature begin to replace urban disassociations; the child relates to the life force of the

Tiny fires dot the beach at Taalung Slung as participants race against the clock in a Fire Building Contest.

creature he or she consumes. Surviving comes to be seen as something other than a desperate struggle for existence as participants come to realize that the knowledge and skills they acquire are skills for living in harmony with the earth, not in opposition to it.

Fire Building Contest

A fire building contest makes an excellent opening day camp activity. Few youngsters possess even the most rudimentary knowledge of proper fire building, even though it is one of the earliest skills known to humans. A fire building contest serves not only to teach safe and effective techniques, it also instills confidence right from the start for participants considering the Solo/Vision Quest later in the camp program.

A safe location must be chosen for this activity. A beach, gravel bar along a river, a dirt road bed, or other area free of forest litter or underbrush, is ideal. While bowdrill or flint and steel fire starting methods can be used here, it is probably best to start with kitchen matches so participants don't become too discouraged in their first attempts.

An elder on Stein Rediscovery discusses how to plan a safe and enjoyable expedition through the Stein wilderness.

An instructor demonstrates the necessary steps to successful fire building: 1) choosing a dry site with good ventilation; 2) gathering sufficient good fire starter (spruce pitch, birch bark, dry litter, et cetera); 3) splitting dry kindling and having sufficient dry wood on hand to feed the fire. Common causes of failure in fire building should be discussed, such as: 1) insufficient or improper fire starter; 2) using green or wet wood; 3) not feeding the fire enough wood; 4) feeding the fire too much or too large wood too soon; 5) not allowing air flow around all the wood; 6) not allowing gravity to feed the coals with wood freely falling. There is an old saying: "A fire is like a lion, it needs air to roar."

Once everyone has a basic understanding of fire building, explain the contest. "Okay, now," the instructor begins, "each of you will be given two matches for starting your fire, a small pot of water, a cup, and a tea bag. The first person that can pour me a nice hot cup of tea will be the fire building champion! If you fail with your first two matches I will provide more," the instructor adds, "but only one at a time and each additional match will cost you a minute added to your total contest time."

Technique is more important than speed in winning the contest. Too many matches squandered costs valuable time. It is also not uncommon for the quickest fire builders to accidently dump their tea water and douse their fire. Discuss with the group, at the completion of the contest, how careless haste may mean life or death in a survival situation.

Expeditions

A highlight of each two-week Rediscovery session is a five- to six-day wilderness expedition. This is scheduled midway through the camp session so that participants have become more fully acclimatized to the outdoor environment, and more physically and psychologically prepared for the demands of the outing. No two Rediscovery camps offer the same adventure: expeditions range from coastal backpacking to mountaineering, sea kayaking and lake canoeing to white-water rafting. Expeditions offer the thrill of discovery, the spark of danger, the comfort of comrades, and fun of adventure.

In many respects, the Rediscovery expedition resembles other wilderness-adventure programs where the "demands of the trail" become the common challenge and incentive for personal growth and positive social interaction. There is one important difference, however. Rediscovery believes no one should ever be pushed beyond their limits. There may be some tired, aching muscles and the occasional blister, but an expedition should not become an ordeal. Rather than devising a rope system to quickly conquer an obstacle, a Rediscovery expedition might look for the route animals take, which often lead to interesting places: petroglyphs or pictographs on the canyon walls, the opportunity to sleep in a cave overnight or forage wild foods in a glade at the bottom of a gorge. The landscape is viewed as an ever-changing opportunity for interaction — not a barrier to progress.

Expedition groups take time to observe animals and their habits. There is no fixed schedule, no summit that must be reached. Hiking parties on the west coast of Haida Gwaii sometimes take an entire day to travel a few kilometres. But they've seen the elaborate decoy dance of a pair of sandhill cranes leading them away from a concealed nest. They've spent an hour observing a huge black bear overturn beach boulders in search of purple shore crabs. They've seen otter slide into the sea, a killer whale frolicking close to shore, and an eagle carry a fish back to its young high up in a nest. Perhaps they've also lingered to study tide pools, gather mussels for dinner, and pick seaside plantain for a salad. If someone discovers a particularly good wild-berry patch, that becomes the temporary destination. The object of a Rediscovery hike is to pass through the landscape the way the Indians did — like a fish through the water or a bird through the air, leaving no sign of their passing.

No-trace camping is, in fact, one of the most important lessons of the expedition, but it is not a habit which comes easily to youngsters. Few kids think twice about dropping their candy bar wrappers on the ground in town so why should the trail or water be any different? Inform everyone at the outset that they each have a litter pocket (a front or back pocket of their pants, jacket, or vest) where litter can be stored until it can be disposed of properly (burned or buried in a proper garbage pit). Tell them that a reward will be offered from time to time to anyone possessing the mystery piece of litter. The expedition leader determines beforehand what the mystery litter of the day might be (a gum wrapper, orange peel, cigarette butt, et cetera) and rewards anyone who has picked up those objects. The rewards (an apple, bag of trail mix, handful of peanuts, piece of fruit leather, or jerky) are strong incentives to anyone a few days into an expedition. Eventually a new habit is formed and litter is picked up without thought of reward.

In addition to litter control, other important lessons of no-trace camping need to be taught:

1) How to gather firewood without mutilating or killing trees: If you feel that a fire is justified — and conditions are safe — use only small sticks and brush gathered from the forest floor. Avoid living trees and picturesque dead snags during the search for firewood.

2) How to douse a fire and completely conceal a fire site: Unless the fire burns for many hours, any wood thicker than your thumb is not likely to burn down to ashes. Keep in mind that while dousing washes ashes into the soil, charcoal is pure carbon and will last indefinitely. Fire scars are the most lasting marks of the careless and uninformed camper, dotting every type of terrain from ocean beaches to alpine meadow. If you come upon an old fire-pit, do not hesitate to cover it up.

3) How to establish proper latrines. This is another matter that demands special care. The recommended practice is to find a site at least fifteen meters away from open water where a hole can be dug into the biological disposer layer of soil — the first fifteen to twenty centimeters. Burn toilet paper using a pocket lighter and bury the ash with the waste. After you replace the soil, disguise the site as you would a fire pit.

4) How to dispose of garbage which can attract scavengers: Many so-called "problems" in areas with high wilderness recreation use are the result of careless garbage disposal. Be certain that all organic

A Rediscovery expedition in Colorado's San Luis Valley might begin at the Great Sand Dunes National Monument (above), then climb to the Rockies (below).

Haida Gwaii Rediscovery offers wilderness backpacking and kayaking expeditions (above), while Stikine Rediscovery might offer a raft trip down the Spatsizi and Stikine rivers (below).

garbage is thoroughly burned and buried. Everything else that is packed in should be packed out.

5) How to wash dishes and hair without polluting water sources: Use only biodegradable soap in the wilderness and dispose of it in a drainage pit dug into sand or other porous soil. Do not wash dishes directly in creeks or lakes.

Until fairly recently, wilderness travel was usually of a utilitarian nature, its purpose being something other than recreational. Native Indians passed quietly over the land, leaving little more than broken things to mark their "trails." Quiet, unnoticed travel was a key to survival, whether related to stalking one's dinner or fleeing some other hostile tribe.

One of the best ways to involve a group in restoring a campsite so that there is no trace of passing is to pretend that you are just a few hours ahead of pursuers. "Okay now, before we go," the instructor cautions, "let's all make certain that we're not leaving behind any clues that we've been here. Careful now, even the matted grass where you slept could tip somebody off."

The expedition also plays an important role in personal counselling. The large extended family, social unit of the camp, is divided into smaller (nuclear family–like) groups during the expedition. A senior staff member accompanies a junior guide and three to five participants. The smaller groups allow for an added measure of safety as well as provide a more intimate atmosphere for group sharing.

Health and safety standards observed throughout Rediscovery sessions receive added attention during the expedition. Portable radio-phones allow leaders to stay in communication with each other and with base camp in event of emergency. Each expedition leader must also be skilled in wilderness first aid.

The entire expedition teaches camping, outdoor cooking, and survival skills. Normally all groups camp separately, but in relatively close proximity to one another. A good lesson in sharing can occur toward the end of the expedition when food provisions are running low. Each expedition leader chooses a precious item their group has left (raisins, cocoa, peanut butter, honey, cheese, or freshly caught trout) and tells the participants: "We've got more than they have, let's give some of this food to each of the other groups as a gift." There is usually considerable protest to such careless generosity. What the participants don't realize is that all the other groups are doing the same. A miracle of "loaves and fishes" appears to occur in each camp as food arrives from different sources.

Emergency Survival

A popular activity during the expedition is to simulate an emergency survival situation. A person never knows when they might find themselves lost in the wilderness, a survivor of a shipwreck, canoe capsizing, plane crash, or other disaster. Few people possess the knowledge or skills to deal with these situations, so an emergency survival exercise, rehearsed early on in life, could one day save a life.

On Haida Gwaii's Rediscovery, this activity takes place midway through the backpacking expedition when all the groups are enjoying a day layover before beginning the return hike back to base camp. The added isolation and feelings of being far from help lend themselves well to this exercise. That evening, just before sunset, each hike group heads away from their camp site with only sleeping bags, a few matches, and the clothes they are wearing. "We are all going to have to become survivors tonight," the staff leader warns. "Do you mean something bad is going to happen to us?" a child asks with concern. "Not really," the leader reassures, "but we're going to pretend that it does. What if we were all cruising along the shore here in a boat and a surprise storm or engine failure suddenly put us on these rocks," the leader says, pointing to a jagged headland, "what would we do?" "Call for help!" someone suggests. "That's right, if our marine radiophone was operating and we had time to make a call, that would be the most important priority," the leader continues, "but what if the storm is interfering with the radio transmission and the boat is breaking up in the waves against the rocks?" "We could try swimming to shore," a boy offers. "True, but this water is awfully cold," the instructor adds. "Let's take off our shoes and socks, roll up our pants, and see just how cold it feels. Burr!"

The group wades into the sea up to their calves and feel the numbing cold. While still standing in the water, hypothermia is discussed: what it is; how to recognize the symptoms; and the best treatment for a victim. "Hypothermia is the number one cause of death in the wilderness," the instructor points out. "When you see someone shivering violently, losing the co-ordination of body movements, and talking incoherently, they are in imminent danger of death unless you act very quickly." Treatment of shock, a major hemorrhage, and concussion are also discussed briefly.

"Okay now, here's our situation," the instructor announces. "All of us have made it from the shipwreck to shore alive and we've managed to secure a few dry matches and some sleeping bags, but we're in trouble.

Emergency Survival takes place at sunset to lend a sense of urgency to shelter building — where the "survivors" will spend the night.

210

A Haida boy displays his catch of cutthroat trout and new confidence in his ability to survive in the wilds.

Joe is shivering uncontrollably; Colleen has a four-inch cut on her forearm and is losing blood fast; and I've bruised my head on the rocks and have just now blacked out." At this point the instructor collapses on the group, leaving the participants to act and make decisions. They must treat the injuries on a priority basis, light a fire, and build a shelter — this is where they will spend the night. The instructor may need to regain consciousness from time to time to offer suggestions if the group is floundering and leaderless. At the campfire, the instructor discusses with the youngsters their treatment of the make-believe injuries, and how they plan to handle the imaginary days ahead: direction finding, signal fires, food foraging, snares, deadfalls, and the seven deadly enemies of survival — fear, fatigue, hunger, cold, heat, pain, and losing one's desire to live. The survivors spend the night huddled together in their shelter.

Rabbit Roast

Rabbit Roast provides a primal link with our ancient human past and impresses upon youngsters the extent to which many of us have become disconnected with our food sources. While considerable bush skills are required to fully conduct this exercise, survival skill specialists (available through Rediscovery International) can teach these techniques to most anyone.

Domestic rabbits can be purchased for this activity, though a major element of the lesson is lost via this shortcut. If a source of wild game is available that is disease free and not harbouring parasites dangerous to humans, and if these animals can be taken legally without endangering the wild population, then this exercise should properly begin with capturing the animal.

Participants are first taught how to make snares, deadfalls, and live traps for capturing small game. Careful setting of the traps in areas frequented by these animals will be necessary for success. While waiting for one's catch, there is plenty to do in preparing for the next step. Stone cutting tools must be chipped from chirt, basalt, obsidian, or other suitable rock, in order to have a primitive tool for dressing and skinning the animal. (Novices generally require one and a half to three hours to accomplish their first arrowhead.) A bowdrill must also be fashioned and the proper technique acquired to light a fire. A few hours of practice brings surprising proficiency.

The rabbit, once procured (either from the wild or domestic market), now becomes, the focal point of the exercise. Working in pairs, campers gut and clean one rabbit with their hand-made arrowheads. The animal is skinned using only fingernails and the arrowhead, roasted over the fire started by bowdrill, and eaten. The rabbit fur is then tanned by simply peeling off any meat and softening the hide by working it in the hands. Each participant can then use half of the hide to make a small medicine pouch sewn with sinew and a bone needle, fashioned from the rabbit's leg. The medicine pouch can house each participant's arrowhead to always remind them of this powerful experience, their skills at survival, and their basic relationship to all life.

TUNING IN

Nothing brings children into closer contact with the outdoors than by carefully tuning in to nature's wavelengths. Tuning In exercises help kids adjust their receivers — their senses, heart, body, and mind — to a wavelength different from the ones they are usually tuned in to: television, video games, radio, and school. How does the forest feel lying on one's back under a soft blanket of needles and moss? What is it like to be a tree and feel the full force of a storm or a bird arranging a nest in your branches? How do you record the subtle sounds of nature's orchestra, the hushed rustle of wind in the grass, the sudden swoosh of a raven, the murmur of a night cricket? And how do we perceive our moment in time on this planet; what is our vision for the future? By sharpening our perception, getting rid of other distractions, and focusing on what we feel, see, and sense right around us, we can all become more attuned.

Forest Blankets

A classic acclimatization experience, Forest Blankets appeals to all, even hyperactive youth. Forest Blankets makes for a very nice closing to a forest outing, or as a resting period following a fast game like Hungry, Hungry Marten.

Gather the group together in a forest area with soft moss, deep beds of needles, or leaves forming the forest floor. "We've had an opportunity today to touch, smell, taste, and see the forest in many different ways," the instructor begins, "but now we're going to totally become a part of this ecosystem. We're going to pretend that we are clumps of moss, branches, or leaves that have fallen from the canopy overhead to rest here on the forest floor. We will let our bodies melt into the earth, looking up at the treetops where we've come from, and reflect on what we will again become as we're recycled as nutrients back into the

Peering from beneath a Forest Blanket, a young Haida boy gazes up through the treetops.

ground. There is no life and death here, only renewal," the instructor says. "Even the insects are part of the process: try to relax if one should crawl onto you. Feel its tiny feet moving over your skin." (Apply insect repellent only if mosquitoes and other biting insects are especially annoying.)

Whispering now, the instructor lays down one of the youngsters on their back while all the others help half-bury the person under leaves, needles, branches, or moss. Put just enough weight on the body for it to be noticeable. Hands are especially important areas for direct contact with the forest litter. Try to set an arching branch over the person's eyes with enough leaves or needles on it to create a three-dimensional effect when looking up. Also try to use only forest litter — not living specimens.

Once the first youngster is comfortably tucked away under their forest blanket, move on to a new location in silence, eight to ten metres away, and begin to bury the next volunteer. Eventually, everyone should be lying peacefully out of view of one another and staring up through the treetops.

There is no optimum time period for Forest Blankets. It depends totally on the group. Some will get restless after ten minutes; others will enjoy the experience for nearly an hour or more. Signs of fidgeting or talk should be the instructor's cue to end the exercise.

Pick the participants up in the order they were dropped off. Ask each to describe the experience. Many will talk of the animals they heard: squirrels, songbirds, woodpeckers. Some will have revelations: "Did you know that raindrops fall in spirals?"

One boy in particular had a most memorable experience. A mosquito landed on the moss above his eyes and spread its wings to dry in the sun. Looking through the wings of the mosquito fifty metres up to the treetops, the boy saw an eagle circling in the clearing overhead. Months later in school, an English teacher got to wonder about the title of an essay handed in: "Seeing the World Through the Wings of a Mosquito."

Be A Tree

An active, creative-visualization experience, Be A Tree can be applied to virtually any animal or plant, but works especially well for simulating a tree. A peaceful forest setting with sun streaming through the canopy and a chorus of birds singing would be the ideal environment for this simulation. Failing that, a recording of relaxing music could be used as background sound, even in an enclosed room.

Have all the participants spread out, standing so they have room to move their arms widely in any direction. Now have them take a deep breath, exhale three times, relax, and close their eyes. The instructor's voice is critical to the experience. Speak in a slow, rhythmic, almost hypnotic tone: "Imagine ourselves as a forest of trees. We have been standing together here for a long, long time. Our roots are intricately intertwined, providing us all with mutual support. Feel the presence of your neighbouring trees as you slowly spread out your thick strong roots [toes] to absorb moisture and nutrients from deep in the earth.

"Think now of your trunk, a sold mass of wood at the centre for support and the thin living skin just beneath the bark, through which pass nutrients in the form of sap, from the roots to the leaves. Now slowly spread out your arms, your branches to the sunlight. Let your hands and fingers be your leaves dancing in the breeze.

"Imagine a bird landing on one of your finger branches. You can feel its tiny feet clutching the twig it stands on. You can feel its beak being drawn from side to side over your bark to clean and sharpen it. Now the bird is hopping around, looking for insects under your leaves. It feels good to know that the bird is looking after your health. Perhaps it will

A score from Nature's Orchestra can be musical notes, drawings, colours, or words.

build a nest here, using fallen twigs from your branches and grass that grows near your trunk."

The instructor continues, bringing any number of animals, from squirrels to raccoons, into play. Take the trees through a violent thunderstorm or gale. Dramatic music is especially effective here. Take the trees also on a journey through the four seasons. Let them experience losing all their leaves; the frigid dormancy of winter and the heavy weight of snow and ice; the resurgence of life in the spring, the rising of the sap and the bursting of the buds; and finally the full life of midsummer, photosynthesizing energy from the sun, growing in height and girth — another summer among hundreds represented by a new growth ring.

Creative visualization allows participants insight into other living things they might otherwise never experience. It can also reduce stress, improve a person's sense of well-being, and help them understand their relationships with the natural world.

Nature's Orchestra

How often do youth listen to, or even conceive of, the sounds of nature as music? In a rock-till-you-drop culture, it is not easy to tune into a frog orchestration at dusk, the babble of a brook under a snowbank, or the call of a thrush deep in the forest.

Nature's Orchestra helps put some people more in touch with the oldest music on earth. Any natural setting will suit this activity, as long as it is well removed from human-generated noise.

Once a location is found, give each of the participants a large index card drawn up as a musical-score sheet, but without any notes on it. The participants spread out so that each is alone to record the music they

hear all around them.

At first, most will hear nothing. Then they may pick up on the more obvious sounds: the call of a raven, the chatter of a squirrel, the song of a bird, or the buzz of a bee. The subtle sounds will come more gradually: the whisper of wind in the treetops, the muffled creaking of a trunk, the murmur of a distant creek or seashore, or the scurry of a mouse through forest litter.

Whatever one hears, they are to record. Nature is the composer here, not the student. Those who have a grasp of music may wish to record musical notes on the bars of their score sheet. Others may find it easier to write out phonetically the sounds they hear: swish, swish, swish. Bzzzz zzzzz ... swish, chirp, chirp, ka-chirp.

Little drawings can be used to try distinguishing the source of different sounds. Even a colour spectrum could be employed, ranging from cool to warm colours — blue waves for soft sounds to bold red slashes for loud sounds. The object here is to listen and express the auditory experience as creatively as possible on paper.

This is a very personal experience, perfect for a Spirit Spot. If any would like to share their score sheet with another, they should be encouraged to do so afterward. Otherwise the Nature's Orchestra sheets should be hidden away in each youngster's personally addressed envelope, along with their Spirit Spot drawing and Letter to the Future. Three years after they leave the program, the sounds of their Spirit Spot will arrive in the mail.

Shared Vision

Times of solitude and quiet reflection often provide the best opportunities, not only for seeing one's place in relation to nature, but also in

A young girl composes her feelings, fears, and hopes for the future in Shared Vision.

218

relation to humanity. Shared Vision is an activity ideally suited for the final visit to one's Spirit Spot.

"Today we're going to do something very special," the instructor announces to the group before they go off to their Spirit Spots. "In the past few days, we've had an opportunity to paint or draw impressions from our Spirit Spot. We've recorded the music from our Spirit Spots as part of Nature's Orchestra, and we've all written a confidential Letter to the Future. What we would like you to do today is go back in your mind's eye to imagine the earliest days of our species on this earth. What was life like back then? How did people get along with each other and their environment? Next, we'd like you to think about the present, the here and now. What are your images of the world today? We'd like you to consider what you think the world will be like in the future, based on our history as a species. Will there continue to be war, hatred, racism, famine, overpopulation, environmental destruction, or will we be pursuing a different course?"

The instructor now gives each participant a standard 8 1/2-x-11-inch sheet of paper divided into three equal sections. Each section is titled along the top: My View: Past/Present/Future.

"Remember now," the instructor continues, "each of you is to draw or write out the way you really feel the world was, is, and will be. Now look at the back of your paper. It reads: My Vision. There is a lot of space here, because this is the most important part of all. Here you are to express, not the way you think the world will be, but the way you want it to be. You may draw or write down your ideas, but give it some very careful thought. Remember, this is all our tomorrows we're talking about — the world you want for your children and grandchildren."

It may be necessary to extend the normal time of Spirit Spot so no one feels rushed. When all are called back together, have everyone sit in a circle and pass their papers clockwise from person to person, so all have an opportunity to see how others expressed themselves. When the papers come back around to their owners again, ask if anyone would like to share their thoughts with the group. A good discussion should follow. Most youth are not too optimistic about the future, the way they think it will be. But their visions are clear and positive for the way they want it to be: a world free of poverty, war, and starvation; a world where everyone enjoys good health care and a healthy environment; a world where different nations, races, and religions respect one another's differences and live in peace.

"They say that without a vision you perish," the instructor continues.

"What we need now is more than a personal vision, however, we need a shared vision. Let's all start working toward such a vision right here and now. Everyone pass your vision papers around the circle again — quickly this time. Think of the earth spinning on its axis, hurling us through space at 104,650 kilometres per hour. Think of the planets rotating around our sun and our solar system swirling in our galaxy. Let your visions be as expansive as that whole universe. There are no limits to what we can achieve together. If each of us have it in us to dream of a better world, we have it in us to create one."

The instructor makes sure that no one is holding his or her own paper, then shouts: "Stop! Okay, now we begin our tasks. The person's vision you are holding is part of your vision too. Take that shared vision home with you and start working on it today."

PART III

THE GROWING FAMILY

I know nothing
of great mysteries
know less of creation
I do know
that the farther backward
in time that I travel
the more grandmothers
and the farther forward
the more grandchildren
I am obligated to both

lee maracle
from *I Am Woman*

Hawaiian Rainbow Man Petroglyph

CHAPTER 1
REDISCOVERY INTERNATIONAL

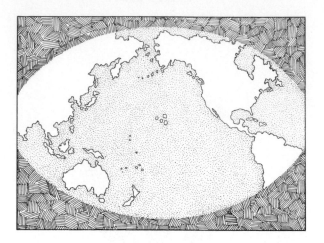

As news of the success of the first Rediscovery camp spread out from the shores of Haida Gwaii, other communities from different cultural backgrounds expressed a desire to develop similar programs. For many years and for obvious reasons, their requests for assistance could not be met by the local Queen Charlotte Islands Rediscovery Society. With the formation of the Rediscovery International Foundation, however, the field experience from the first camp was made available to others, and, within four years, eight Rediscovery camps were in operation.

Rediscovery International Foundation is a federally registered charity which works on three levels: 1) initiating new programs; 2) monitoring and assisting existing programs; and 3) facilitating cross-cultural exchanges between participants from different programs. Program initiation must begin at the community level before Rediscovery International can assist. The Rediscovery International Foundation's board of directors are determined to see that their efforts serve to further empower local communities in their programs, rather than lead to a dependency on the international support body.

The following Rediscovery camps are presented here in the order in which they developed, and in the words of people closely associated with their development and ongoing operations.

It is with pride that Rediscovery International is associated with this growing family of camps, and all the people involved.

HAIDA GWAII REDISCOVERY
By *Michael Nicholl and Robert Davis*

Michael Nicholl is Haida, and the chairman of the board of the Queen Charlotte Island's Natural and Cultural History Rediscovery Society. Robert (Pedro) Davis is a young Haida man, and member of the Kun'laanaas family of the Raven Clan.

The Rediscovery camp on the west coast of Haida Gwaii (Queen Charlotte Islands) is undergoing a dramatic period of growth. For our first decade, we were essentially a summer tent camp. Now, three Haidanaas (longhouses) sit facing the open reaches of the Pacific Ocean. These longhouses provide year-round shelter for an expanding operation which will include fall and spring Alcohol and Drug Sessions. We are also initiating discussion to provide an innovative educational approach which would become a regular part of the local school curriculum. Before such substantial growth can occur, Rediscovery must secure adequate funds to complete our expansion, which includes a ceremony and feast house, a bathhouse, and a totem pole. Following this, Rediscovery will host a house-naming ceremonial potlatch, marking the rebirth of a Haida village, the first in well over a century. Individuals who make substantial donations will be invited to what should be the biggest potlatch held in living memory, a testimony to our common belief in the strength and future of our children.

That future is reflected in the words of Robert Davis as he recounts his experiences on Haida Gwaii Rediscovery in the summer of 1988, during a trial Alcohol and Drug Program: "I was happy to get away because I was really getting into booze and drugs around here. It was coming to a point where I wanted to do it every day. When I heard the plane, I was so excited but we had to take the second plane.

"When I got out there, it was hard to adjust, but when I did it, it was just like home away from home. I made a lot more friends out there. It was just like we all turned into one big family. I learned this when we had our good days and bad days.

"When we started the program I didn't think anything about it but it took me a while to learn that I was doing a bit too much alcohol and drugs. It took one person to change that. He made me open right up to him. His name was Rick and practically every time I had him in my group, he told me things I didn't know about him and I told him about me and my alcohol and drug problem, and I cried because it was the first time I told anybody about my past.

"There was one other time when I cried and that was when my parents came out to see what we do out at Rediscovery. When they got out there, I was surprised because I didn't know if they were coming out. When they did, I helped them over to Lepas Bay. They were out there for three days. On the second day, I told them about my alcohol and drug problem.

"The hike is the best part of Rediscovery. It is a challenge and lots of fun! When we started it was like we were leaving home for good. It was raining all the way to Sialun Bay, so we stayed there. When we got there, the participants usually make supper and we had spaghetti and it was hot, hot, spaghetti. We put four tablespoons of hot pepper in it. The next day we went down to Beresford for lunch. Then we came back to camp.

"Ceremony Night is one night I won't forget, because it was the best night I had out there. Everybody was happy and I felt a change in my life about using drugs and alcohol. I felt I didn't need it anymore. I would recommend Rediscovery because it does help people change their lives."

Haida Gwaii Rediscovery Society
Box 684
Masset, Haida Gwaii
Via Canada Post
VOT 1M0
Telephone: (604) 626-5460

Participants kayak-surf on beautiful Taalung Slung bay and backpack six days along the shores of Duu Guusd, Haida Tribal Park.

Letting go of the schedule and having fun with friends is part of the secret to Haida Gwaii Rediscovery's success.

REDISCOVERY FOUR CORNERS
By Lorraine Fox Davis

Lorraine Fox Davis is a native of Cree and Blackfoot ancestry who founded Rediscovery Four Corners in Colorado, and has served as administrator and program director since 1985.

Rediscovery Four Corners, in south central Colorado, was the first Rediscovery camp to develop beyond Haida Gwaii. The program was founded in 1985 with the guidance of Lakota, Pueblo, and Southern Ute elders. Rediscovery Four Corners is incorporated as a non-profit foundation, with a broad-based board of directors comprised of respected Native American leaders, recreation specialists, and business professionals.

Located in the Four Corners region of the southwestern United States (Colorado, New Mexico, Arizona, and Utah), Rediscovery Four Corners takes its name from the crossroads of these states. The name is also indicative of the four directions held sacred by all indigenous peoples, and of the coming together of young people of the four races. The campsite is located at the base of the Sangre de Cristo mountain range in the San Luis Valley. South of the camp, 4,200-metre Mount Blanca rises majestically, considered by the indigenous people of the area to be the first of the four sacred mountains.

The valley below camp is home to coyote, bobcat, bear, antelope, deer, and eagles, with bighorn sheep and mountain goat at higher elevations. The camp is situated at 2,490 metres elevation, in an open meadow of sage and native grass on Wild Cherry Creek, surrounded by pinon pine and juniper trees. Aspen and cottonwood follow the creek to alpine lakes.

Participants and staff live in a cluster of Plains-style tipis, surrounding a central fire pit. Cooking and daily chores are shared by all at the large outdoor cooking pit and kitchen area near the stream. Drawn together in a family atmosphere, the groups come from a wide range of native cultures, including Lakota, Pueblo, Ute, Navajo, and Arapahoe, as well as from non-native backgrounds.

Having traditional American Indian elders share their wisdom and skills with the young people and lead them in ceremony and prayers is often a profound and cherished experience. One boy who had never participated in traditional ceremonies said that being in the sweat lodge with an elder was the best part of the program for him. He spoke of his fear, and how everything seemed different and more beautiful after the ceremony. A Navajo girl said that taking part in ceremonies of other tribes helped her appreciate her own culture even more. A broad intertribal and cross-cultural bond is formed by many participants, leading them to greater appreciation, understanding, and respect. In describing the program, a director for the Navajo division of Save the Children said, "The importance of this camp is that it positively reinforces the ideals of our forefathers' love of nature and respect for all living things, instilling their ideals within our youth." Gary Collins, chairman of the Northern Arapahoe Business Council, said, "Rediscovery is structured to have elders and youth coming together to share knowledge and wisdom. They emphasize the ways of the old and want to see these passed from generation to generation."

Despite a lack of public funding, Rediscovery Four Corners not only operates a successful program, but has been able to assist other U.S. regions in developing programs in their area. In 1987 and 1988, the staff of Rediscovery Four Corners assisted the Joint Tribal Councils of the Northern Arapahoe and Shoshone in the establishment of the Wind River Rediscovery. Plans are now underway for Rediscovery Four Corners to help develop programs to serve Indian youth of Denver and the Front Range area of Colorado.

Rediscovery Four Corners
Box 100
Crestone, Colorado
U.S.A. 81131
Telephone: (719) 256-4474

The setting for Rediscovery Four Corners camp in southern Colorado includes Great Sand Dunes National Monument backed by Sangre de Cristo mountains.

Rediscovery Four Corners in the San Luis Valley is a cluster of Plains Indian tipis at the 2,490-metre elevation, while expeditions climb much higher.

STEIN REDISCOVERY
By Jessoa Lightfoot

Jessoa Lightfoot has been involved with Stein Rediscovery since it began in 1986. She now works as program co-ordinator. As a resident of Lytton for nineteen years, Jessoa became involved in Stein Rediscovery after meeting the local native elders and learning of their respect for the land.

My burning feet run over the hot sandy flat, dotted with prickly cactus, sage, and tumbled rocks, to cool in the Stein River. Here at the mouth, I face a wall of red to the east. North to south runs the Fraser River, and back, westward through the mountains, runs the Stein River. A mile or so upstream, I pause by a pictograph and say my prayer. Through open pine forest, I go on a trail thousands have walked. As the canyon narrows, I climb over rock slide, sometimes cooled, when the trail dips to a shady cedar grove. In early summer, wild strawberries — in fall, mushrooms add to my nourishment. The river is always near, tumbling over rocks, pools of fish throughout. So might the experience be for a Rediscovery participant on their first day's hike into the Stein Valley.

Located just one-hundred-sixty kilometres northeast of Vancouver, the Stein watershed is home to the Stein Rediscovery program. Since its formation in 1986, the Stein Natural and Cultural Heritage Rediscovery Society has brought together native and non-native youth (ages twelve to nineteen) to explore and discover the natural and cultural worlds of this area. For urban teenagers, Stein Rediscovery may be their first chance to get out of the city. Before heading into the Stein Valley, Lisa Kirk, an eighteen-year-old from Vancouver, said, "I think it's going to be really different and beautiful. I've never been in a forest before." Some participants begin their hike in the alpine areas at the western or northern edges of the watershed. The group works together to cover up to eighty kilometres of trail in the next two weeks. Along the way they find alpine flowers, mountain lakes, and magnificent views stretching across wide horizons. Younger participants hike thirty-five kilometres from the mouth to the base camp, where all participants spend a portion of their time. Located at the confluence of Cottonwood Creek and the Stein, nestled into the forest on the banks of the river, a circle of tipis surrounds the sacred fire.

Just upstream a traditional sweat lodge is ready for use. Here, local elders join the youth to share their skills and stories.

Each day in base camp begins with a rabbit run through the forest and a bird dip in the cold river. Chores are shared by all. Day hikes, survival skills, wild plant identification, swimming, basketry, volleyball, leather work, games that illustrate the interdependence of life — all these activities fill the days in base camp. After evening meal the group forms a circle at the fire, sharing the day's events, past stories, future dreams.

As the session draws to an end, participants who wish go on a twenty-four-hour solo. The sweat lodge helps prepare the youth for their time alone. The Stein Valley has traditionally been used by native youth for Spirit Quest. The continuation of this tradition through Rediscovery has tremendous significance to those who take part. A special Feast and Ceremony honours the soloists on their return.

All too soon it is time to pack up and hike the trail out to Lytton. Through the exertion on the trail, the sharing of responsibilities, the play, the quiet times alone, the caring of the elders, a sensitivity grows. This sensitivity results in a respect for culture, other people, and oneself that will last a lifetime.

Stein Rediscovery is a federally registered charity and will issue tax receipts for donations of $5 or more. Sponsorship of less fortunate participants is made possible by your support.

Stein Rediscovery
Box 195
Lytton, B.C.
Canada V0K 1Z0
Telephone: (604) 455-2757

Stein Rediscovery leads participants on expeditions which traverse the Stein watershed (above) and offers a Solo Vision/Quest with traditional sweat lodge and the guidance of native elders (below).

A senior guide points to the bend in the Stein River where the base camp is located, in the heart of the Stein wilderness.

WIND RIVER REDISCOVERY

Located on the Wind River Reservation in western Wyoming, Wind River Rediscovery is sponsored by the Joint Tribal Councils of the Shoshone and Northern Arapahoe of Wind River. The camp lies in Washakie Park, beautiful mountainous country near Moccasin Lake. The core staff of Rediscovery Four Corners from Colorado served as consultants and trainers of the Wind River staff to help launch this new Rediscovery in 1987. This marks the first time that a Rediscovery camp has devoted its time and resources to help establish a sister program.

Camp facilities combine Plains Indian tipis and log cabins. Activities at Wind River Rediscovery include rock climbing, backpacking, canoeing, native games, arts and crafts. Tribal councilmen, elders, spiritual leaders of both the Northern Arapahoe and the Shoshone nations teach food gathering along the trail during a four-day backpack expedition into the high country. Bear sightings are common in the remote parts of the reservation and fishing is excellent. Families of campers, elders, and councilmen attend a feast and award ceremony featuring a traditional *giveaway*.

Wind River Rediscovery plans to incorporate Northern Arapahoe and Shoshone language training into the program, as well as teach participants about tribal government and the sovereign rights of Indian nations. Renewed cultural pride and increased self-esteem are much in evidence when tribal councilmen interview participants returning from the camp. "It made me feel good about myself," one girl said with conviction. Meeting new friends, accepting new challenges, and increased independence sustained her interest in the camp and sparked confidence in her abilities. Wind River also intends to increase elder involvement and hold exchange programs in the future.

Wind River Rediscovery
c/o Joint Tribal Councils of the Shoshone and Arapahoe of Wind River
Box 655
Ethete, Wyoming
U.S.A. 82520
Telephone: (307) 332-6120

Balance War games (above) and backpacking expeditions (below) are popular with the Arapahoe and Shoshone youth at Wind River Rediscovery.

238

*Plains tipis and log cabins provide the camp facilities in this remote
part of the Wind River Reservation (above), where elders gather to
share in a feast and bless the food (below).*

239

CHAKO KUNAMOKST REDISCOVERY
By Kent Danielson

Kent Danielson is the current president of Chako Kunamokst Rediscovery Society, and is married to Barbara (Suunders) Danielson of Nuxalk ancestry, who was the project co-ordinator in 1987-88. He is a dental therapist by trade, whose chief obsession is photography.

At first glance, the Bella Coola visitor sees a land of dramatic superlatives, a maze of deep inlets, towering mountains, and hanging glaciers. Waterfalls and rivers cascade to the sea, segmenting the rich canopy of cedar, fir, and cottonwood. Few earthly places can match the rich natural and cultural heritage of Bella Coola's first citizens, the Nuxalk people.

Over the past generation, this community has suffered many social problems. The damage has hit hardest with the youth — depression leading to suicide, sexual abuse and the loss of self-worth, family violence, lack of constructive recreation, crime .... The list is long; the pain is deep. The community has responded with a variety of programs and treatments. The most recent and perhaps the most comprehensive is the Chako Kunamokst Rediscovery project.

Chako Kunamokst means *a gathering place* in the Chinook trade language of the northwest coast. The purpose of the project is to bring together Nuxalk elders, other suitable role models, and youth, both native and non-native, in a safe wilderness environment to facilitate learning, healing, and respect. The pilot project was initiated by the Bella

Coola Community Support Society in the summer of 1986. The "gathering" took place at the Kimsquit Indian Reserve. Its location has proved ideal for the project's purposes. Isolated, rich with history and natural beauty, Kimsquit has since become the home for our annual summer camp sessions. The participants come from throughout the central coast of British Columbia. Each day begins with a Sunrise Greeting, a Four Direction Run, Morning Purification in the Dean River, followed by a Circle Hug. Participants gain insight into Nuxalk culture through the living words of the elders and the ancient links with the past — petroglyphs along the river canyon, the old burial grounds, and longhouse ruins. Highlights of the two-week sessions include a canoe expedition down the Dean Channel to a site near Alexander Mackenzie's historic termination of his trans-Canada expedition, exploring burial caves, hot springs, and hidden lakes en route. Encounters with the area's abundant wildlife — bears, whales, eagles — etch in each participant's mind a sense of awe and reverence for the environment.

Chako Kunamokst Rediscovery Society has gone beyond offering just the Kimsquit summer camps. A delegation of youth and elders, supported by the project, participated in the reviving of the Traditional Grease Trail Gathering at Tanya Lakes with the Ulcatcho and Nazcho people. Youth conferences, weekend workshops, and training sessions have extended what was once a summer program to a year-round endeavour. Some of the issues presented are youth peer leadership, substance abuse, suicide prevention, and peer counselling, to name a few. A delegation of Nuxalk youth and elders attended the tenth-anniversary celebration of Rediscovery on Haida Gwaii. This exchange of ideas left an indelible impression on all. Behind all these programs lie hours and hours of volunteer help. Our chief benefactor has been British Columbia's Mental Health Service, providing operational funds, and the Vancouver Foundation, which contributed toward our capital expenditures. Chako Kunamokst Rediscovery Society is actively recruiting more members to both share the load and the joys of Rediscovery.

Chako Kunamokst Rediscovery
Box 747, Bella Coola, B.C.
Canada V0T 1C0
Telephone: (604) 799-5525

Bella Coola youth build a team pyramid on a river bar at Chako Kunamokst Rediscovery (above) and learn traditional cedar bark basketry as part of Nuxalk cultural lessons (below).

Kimsquit Reserve at the mouth of the Dean River is an ancient Nuxalk village site and the setting for today's Chako Kunamokst Rediscovery.

HEILTSUK REDISCOVERY
By Frank Brown

Frank Brown is a Heiltsuk of Bella Coola who completed Capilano College's Outdoor Recreation Management course and the "Glwa" project — the carving of a traditional Heiltsuk ocean-going canoe, which he led on an expedition from Bella Bella to Expo 86 in Vancouver. Frank also serves as founder and program director of Heiltsuk Rediscovery.

The Heiltsuk Nation has inhabited the central coast of what is now British Columbia for the past ten thousand years. For the past one hundred years, we have been dealing with many social and economic obstacles, all of which seriously undermine the potential and promise of our youth. However, through our local Rediscovery program, we are addressing these problems. We are relearning the ancient laws of our ancestors through our special relationship with the land, which has sustained our mental, emotional, spiritual, and physical well-being since time immemorial. An ancient lesson we are sharing with our community youth through the Heiltsuk Rediscovery program is the importance of the land to our culture, for without the land, we have no culture.

The following process to self-actualization has been incorporated into the Heiltsuk Rediscovery. It is based on my experience, when, at the age of fourteen, I was by myself in the wilderness for almost a year. In past ages, within indigenous cultures, a young person about to become an adult went through rites-of-passage ceremonies in order to become an adult. I experienced a contemporary version of this process, in which a youth is left alone on the land, and enters the ancient realm of the supernatural world: "In the last days, old men shall dream dreams, and young men shall have visions." There are three stages in rites-of-passage: separation, transition, and incorporation. This is correct from a theoretical point of view. However, from practical experience, I have recognized four sub-stages: 1. Problem State: Emotionally tortured and angry person. 2. Problem Acknowledgement: Purification, and first contact with the natural and supernatural world. 3. Problem Confronted: Facing spiritual self. 4. Accomplishment: Rebirth of the Winalha "Warrior Going Forward" Spirit.

The Heiltsuk people have demonstrated, through community donations and 8,000 volunteer hours in the construction of our traditional bighouse on Goose Island, that when an opportunity exists for positive and productive development, the community acts in co-operation to further the social and spiritual development of its members. As well as the bighouse, we have incorporated Glwa into our Rediscovery. Glwa is an ocean-going canoe which was carved in Bella Bella then paddled to Vancouver for Expo 86. Young people paddled Glwa thirty-five miles before arriving at Heiltsuk Rediscovery on Goose Island.

Within the last decade there has been a social, economic, and political renaissance within the Native Indian population. The general public has, for the most part, been unaware of this, and continues its negative and prejudicial social stereotyping of the native Indian. The Rediscovery program, through multicultural participation, acts against these entrenched attitudes and ideas.

Our Rediscovery program marks a very important point in Heiltsuk history because it symbolizes a time of reflection and transition in our ceremonial and cultural revival. Rediscovery is a verification of our cultural virility, shown through relearning, adaptation, and development of new and innovative cultural and ceremonial traditions. These new directions are very important in sustaining our race, and are presented in a spirit of the preservation and perpetuation of indigenous culture. *To lose a ceremony, is to lose the past. To create a ceremony, is to create a future.*

Heiltsuk Rediscovery
c/o Heiltsuk Band Council
Box 880, Waglisla, B.C.
Canada V0T 1Z0
Telephone: (604) 957-2381

A baby killer whale surfaces beside Glwa, the traditional ocean-going canoe used on Heiltsuk Rediscovery.

Heiltsuk men launch the dugout canoe from Bella Bella (above) for the journey to remote Goose Island, where youth and staff gather in front of a newly erected bighouse (below).

SLIAMMON REDISCOVERY
By Elizabeth Harry

Elizabeth Harry was born and raised in Squirrel Cove, on Cortez Island. She is fluent in her native tongue of Mainland Comox of the Coast Salish Group. Elizabeth is skilled in basket weaving and doll making. The material she works with are cedar bark, wild cherry bark, cedar sapling, and raffia.

For Elizabeth Harry, the project co-ordinator and team leader, her time at Apookum was a treat and personal time of happiness. She was pleased "to be able to go back in time ... and get away from modern living." She believes that our children desperately need the kind of teaching Rediscovery offers if we are to keep the Salish culture and language alive.

The Sliammon Rediscovery project, sponsored by the Sliammon Indian Band, began operating in August 1988. Sliammon is a reserve of approximately six hundred Coast Salish people located four miles north of Powell River in Georgia Strait, one hundred miles north of Vancouver, British Columbia.

The Sliammon Rediscovery camp is established in Homfray Channel at "Apookum" (Forbes Bay, near the mouth of Toba Inlet). Apookum, which means "full of maggots" in Salish, is an ancient food-gathering site that belongs to the Klahoose Band of Indians of Cortez Island.

All participants in the first year were from the Sliammon reserve, but in future the band wants to include children from other ethnic backgrounds as well as from other areas.

Sliammon Rediscovery aims to create a positive cultural experience for participants. This year there were legends and history told, as well as demonstrations in doll weaving and some language.

Sliammon Rediscovery participants hike and gather traditional food (clams, oysters, salmon, and other bottom fish, wild greens and berries). A daily schedule sets aside time for a morning run and river bath before breakfast, group chores, spirit spot, daily outings, and campfires devoted to personal growth and cultural awareness. A four-day forty-mile canoe trip to the "kwek tich nem" (Brem River, midway up Toba Inlet), teaches survival skills, group team building, and offers excellent opportunities for nature study and to learn Indian names for all the coves, bays, and where the traditional fishing grounds are located.

A unique aspect of the Sliammon Rediscovery is a traditional Salish welcoming ceremony. Participants are met on arrival at the beach, and are cleansed by being swept with cedar boughs. It is the belief of the Salish that cedar possesses a medicinal content which wards off undesirable spirits.

For many Salish youth, the Sliammon Rediscovery project is the first real immersion into their culture — learning the "old ways" from the elders, living off the land and sea, and also learning the importance of community and group co-operation.

Sliammon Rediscovery
c/o Sliammon Indian Band Council
R.R. 2, Sliammon Rd.
Powell River, B.C.
V8A 4Z3
Telephone: (605) 483-9646

Evan Adams

A young Coast Salish boy from Sliammon proudly displays a traditional blanket he has woven.

Terry Galligus

Terry Galligus

Sliammon Rediscovery participants help prepare a meal (above) at the tent camp up Homfray Channel (below).

WUNSKAW WILDERNESS CAMP
By Alice Martin

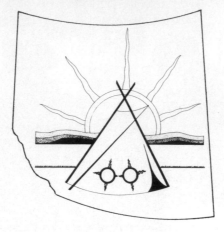

Alice Martin was one of the people that shared the dream and volunteered her time and planning on the board of directors of Wunskaw Wilderness Camp until the position of camp director was available. Alice is originally from Fort Chipewyan and is a treaty Cree. Her husband and two children now live in Anzac, and all of them, as well as her mother, were involved in both camps.

One person had a dream of developing a camp that would be like the old ways. This dream was shared with the people of the area, and it was found that others also had the same dream. In March 1987, five small, isolated communities in northeastern Alberta joined together to develop a program for youth that would encourage the survival of the individual, the community, the native culture, and of nature and all living things.

The result of their efforts and the co-operation of the Community Services Staff from the Municipal Region of the Improvement District 18(N), was the development of the Wunskaw Wilderness Camp for native and non-native youth.

Wunskaw (a Cree word meaning awakening) Wilderness Camp serves a large, sparsely populated region of northeastern Alberta that contains the communities of Fort Chipewyan, Fort McKay, Anzac, Janvier, and Conklin. Community members in this district are predominantly native with Cree, Chipewyan, and Métis ancestry. The communities each have less than three hundred residents, except for Fort Chipewyan, which has

252

approximately twelve hundred residents.

The environment ranges in diversity from Canadian Shield country in the north around Fort Chipewyan to muskeg forests in the southern area. Unique landforms include the Peace/Athabasca delta, the sand dunes, and the tar sands, which can be found along many river banks. Most of the lakes are fly-in only, and many boast of trophy fishing and natural habitats for bald eagle, moose, and beaver.

Due to the large size and diversity of the region, choosing a location for the camp involved designating one northern site and one southern site. Traditionally, the Cree and Chipewyan people were nomadic, and every effort was made to combine the essence of the nomadic tradition by recreating a "summer" fishing camp at both sites. Both tipis and trapper's tents were used in respect for the lifestyle of the Métis trappers and the Indian fishermen and hunters.

Camp I was developed for eight- to eleven-year-olds and was located at Crow Lake, approximately 120 kilometres south of Fort McMurray. This location was chosen for the highway, and a cabin was there for the children if bad weather persisted. Camp II was developed for twelve- to seventeen-year-olds and was intended to be isolated and very primitive. This camp was located at Wylie Lake, 80 kilometres northeast of the community of Fort Chipewyan. Wylie Lake was chosen for its "extreme location," sandy beaches, and good fishing.

For many of the children and youth, it was the first time that they had been away from home and the first chance that they had to go in a sweat lodge and begin to understand the teachings about their native heritage.

"We learned about the culture and how to treat the woman that you love." — Rusty Woodward, age fourteen, Anzac

"I enjoyed the songs we sang, and when you pray hard enough, the spirits will help you." — Early Faichney, age twelve, Fort McKay

Funding for the program was obtained through Improvement District 18(N), Recreation North Leadership Development Association, and the local community recreation societies. All equipment was donated by local Indian bands, community schools, and individuals. Recreation North Leadership Development Association and many individuals from each community have committed their time and energy to build a cultural "future" for their children through Wunskaw Wilderness Camp.

Wunskaw Wilderness Camp
c/o Improvement District 18(N)
513 West Tower Provincial Building, 9915 Franklin Ave.
Fort McMurray, Alberta, Canada T9H 2K4

Cree youth gather around the fire in Northern Alberta for story-telling by an elder (above), and fish for pike in Wylie Lake as the midnight sun nears the horizon (below), at Wunskaw Wilderness Camp.

A young Hawaiian boy blows his puu shell above Kauai's beautiful and ancestral Kallalal Valley.

DEVELOPING REDISCOVERY PROGRAMS

There are a number of regions that have taken the initial steps in developing Rediscovery programs, but which are not yet fully operative. Sometimes local politics, inadequate community support, lack of finances or a sponsoring body, or an inability to secure a suitable location can hamper the development of a Rediscovery-affiliated camp. A few developing programs are briefly described here to acknowledge their endeavours to date and to solicit support for their ultimate success.

STIKINE REDISCOVERY

The community of Iskut in the wilderness of northwest British Columbia has been working toward developing a Rediscovery for a number of years. In 1986, the Iskut band council sponsored the Spatsizi Youth Project, a series of white-water-rafting expeditions down the upper Spatsizi and Stikine rivers. The project served Tahltan and non-native youth from Iskut, Telegraph Creek, and other British Columbia communities. Tahltan participants on the expedition had the rare opportunity to visit their ancestral hunting grounds, old villages sites, and abandoned trading posts. They also hiked onto the Spatsizi Plateau, considered the Serengeti of North America for its concentration of caribou, moose, wolves, and grizzly bear.

The Spatsizi Youth Project benefited from a Rediscovery International Foundation adviser who took part in the first expedition. The hope now is to expand the community-support base of the program by drawing together resources from Iskut, Telegraph Creek, Dease Lake, and Stewart, along with other small northern communities separated by hundreds of miles of wilderness. In addition to rafting expeditions, organizers want to incorporate a base camp into the program of the Spatsizi Youth Project to more fully involve the Tahltan elders.

Spatsizi Youth Project/Stikine Rediscovery
c/o Iskut Band Council
Iskut, B.C.
Canada V0J 1K0
Telephone: (604) 234-3331

REDISCOVERY HAWAII

For several years, members of the Aloha Aina (Love of the Land) Society and the Hawaiian Farmers of Hanalei Inc. have been pursuing a cultural awareness program for youth on the Hawaiian island of Kauai. Maka Makanani and David Sproat, natives of Hawaiian ancestry, have been working to bring this program to fruition, but they face the obstacles of finding the necessary funds and a suitable location.

Once operative, Rediscovery Hawaii will reflect Hawaiian culture in many ways. Traditional pili-grass-thatched dwellings will serve as camp facilities. Kupunas (Hawaiian elders) will be central to the extended Polynesian family camp structure. Traditional Hawaiian games and skills will be taught in three distinct settings:

1. Maikai *(toward the sea)*: A focus on traditional fishing techniques (net throwing, fish ponds, and weirs), on the construction and use of traditional Polynesian sea craft, and on traditional sports such as surfing and skin diving.

2. Kula *(the valley farmlands)*: A focus on wet and dry land taro production, traditional horticulture, tropical fruit propagation, and rearing of Polynesian domestic animals (pigs and dogs).

3. Mauka *(toward the mountains)*: A focus on the endemic flora and fauna of the Hawaiian archipelago, reforestation of native trees, propagation of Kauai's rare and endangered species, harvesting edible and medicinal plants, and learning traditional healing.

Already, Haida youth from Rediscovery on Haida Gwaii have taken part in hiking and camping adventures with their Hawaiian hosts on Kauai. There are exciting prospects of further cultural exchanges between the first peoples of the Pacific and others.

Rediscovery Hawaii
c/o Maka Makanani
323 Kamokicai Rd.
Kapaa, Kauai
Hawaii 96746
Telephone: (808) 822-5184

CHEANUH REDISCOVERY

Cheanuh Bay, also known as Becher Bay, on the southern end of British Columbia's Vancouver Island, is an ancient Indian site with a 14,000-year history of occupation. Here, the Becher Bay Indian Band, supported by many southern Vancouver Island bands, hopes to develop a year-round Rediscovery camp. The climate, tempered by Pacific currents, creates one of the only locations in Canada suitable for year-round summer camp activities. The proximity of Cheanuh Bay to major population centres — Seattle, Vancouver, and Victoria — also provides opportunities for the camp to serve the needs of urban youth in crisis. Perhaps the most exciting prospect of all for Cheanuh

A Tahltan boy serenades fellow campers from the porch of a trapper's cabin in the Stikine wilderness (above), while two girls don wildflower headbands for a Ceremony Night on Stikine Rediscovery.

A Kwakiutl totem pole emerges out of the fog in the ancestral homeland where Port Hardy Rediscovery will be located.

Rediscovery is the potential of involving the world community through the Lester Pearson World College of the Pacific — a close neighbour to the proposed campsite. One of seven United World colleges, this school hosts students aged seventeen to nineteen from all nations. Six students from Japan, Hong Kong, Costa Rica, Canada, and the U.S.A. have already taken part in pilot Cheanuh Rediscovery sessions.

Cheanuh Rediscovery
c/o Evelyn Armstrong
1120 Kiwi Rd.
Victoria, B.C.
Canada V9B 5C1
Telephone: (604) 474-6345

PORT HARDY REDISCOVERY

Another new and exciting Rediscovery program is developing on the northern tip of Canada's Vancouver Island. Sponsored by the Port Hardy Crisis Centre, Port Hardy Rediscovery draws together a broad range of community members, ranging from concerned parents and social workers to band administrators and probation officers. In addition, a Council of Elders of the Kwakiutl Nation helps to oversee and advise in program development.

The campsite being considered is on Gilford Island, a traditional habitation and food-gathering site for the Kwakiutl. The waters surrounding Gilford Island and nearby Robson Bight are world-famous as the summer home of the largest concentration of killer whales. The Killer Whale and Thunderbird figure prominently in Kwakiutl mythology and will be among the many crests displayed in totems, dance screens, and the house frontal of a traditional longhouse proposed for the camp location. The rich ceremonial life for which the Kwakiutl are world-renowned will bring a distinction to this camp unlike any other.

Port Hardy Rediscovery
c/o Port Hardy Crisis Centre
P.O. Box 2446
Port Hardy, British Columbia
Canada V0N 2P0
Telephone: (604) 949-8333

CHAPTER 2
DEVELOPING A REDISCOVERY OF YOUR OWN

One of the most common inquiries the Rediscovery International Foundation receives is: "Can you set up a Rediscovery program in our community?" The answer is always the same, a qualified "No." Rediscovery International was not established to franchise programs, but to help communities develop their own. The foundation believes that unless people determine their own needs, call on their own resources, and implement their own programs, that the unique character of a community, the local culture, and natural-history features may not be properly reflected. Rediscovery encourages diversity between its affiliated camps and that diversity begins at the community level.

Each Rediscovery camp depends on a community pulling together and making a concerted effort to launch their program and keep it operating. Given the nature of local politics and a general lack of funds, this is more often than not a herculean task. The achievements of Rediscovery reflect thousands of volunteer hours and generous contributions of people at the local level. Their dedication and effort not only draw the community much closer together, but clearly demonstrates to the youth of those communities that somebody cares.

Often an existing society, charitable organization, Indian band (or tribal council) will agree to act as a sponsor in starting up a Rediscovery camp — especially for the first year or two of operation. Thereafter, it is not uncommon for the original sponsoring body to incorporate Rediscovery as a distinct society with its own board and administration.

Usually, this original sponsoring body will invite a representative of Rediscovery International to address representatives of the local community: native elders, band/tribal administrators and elected officials, social workers, probation officers, public health workers, family support counsellors, schoolteachers, parents, ministers/priests, police officers, service clubs, and local businesses. A real effort should be made to attract youth to these meetings as well, for they often better express their real needs than agencies or professionals.

Films and slide presentations of existing Rediscovery camps convey a contagious enthusiasm; often a single presentation by a Rediscovery International representative can bridge divisions in the most fractured communities and draw people together in a single purpose. The following outline was designed to help communities clarify their vision, and consider the many facets of developing a Rediscovery of their own.

GUIDELINES FOR ESTABLISHING A REDISCOVERY
Phase I: Conceptual
A. What are the specific needs of your community?
   Possible needs may include:
   — providing an alternative for youth at risk.
   — counselling youth in crisis.
   — bridging the generation gap between youth and elders.
   — promoting health and fitness in an alcohol/drug free environment.
   — developing social responsibility through co-operative activities.
   — training in survival and outdoor skills, including traditional native technologies.
   — contributing to a greater sense of pride in one's culture and in one's own accomplishments.
   — providing opportunities for cross-cultural understanding in a social family context.
   — rekindling an interest in education for school drop-outs.
   — providing leadership training and communication skills.
   — assisting youth in the transition to adulthood through rites of passage.
B. Who will be the target group?
C. Who will act as the sponsoring society or organization?
D. Where will the program be located?

New friendships are only one of the many benefits of a Rediscovery camp. Nuxalk and non-native youth and staff embrace in a morning Circle Hug at Chako Kunamokst Rediscovery.

E. What facilities will be required to meet the needs of the camp?

F. What will be the criteria for participant selection?

G. What will be the criteria for staff selection?

H. What funding sources will be approached — public and private?

Phase II: Pre-operational

A. Solicit community support.

B. Design a written program proposal (including letters of community support) and prepare a visual package to support your document.

C. Submit the program proposal to all relevant agencies for support, moral and financial.

D. Hire an administrator as soon as possible to secure funds and co-ordinate the program. Consider this a year-round position.

E. Circulate information on your program to all relevant agencies in your community and districts, as well as to the schools.

F. Purchase equipment. Invest in quality, and label everything.

G. Begin facility development.

H. Train and upgrade skills for staff where necessary, prior to hiring. Staff positions may include: program director/camp supervisor/ elders/senior guides/camp cook/junior guides.

I. Establish the line of command between staff and the sponsoring organization and be certain that all employees clearly understand it.

J. Secure liability insurance.

K. Have the camp inspected and approved by all regulatory bodies in your region.

L. Establish communications between camp and the nearest community, and rehearse emergency procedures.

M. Select participants. Rediscovery-affiliated programs do not discriminate on the basis of race, sex, creed, culture, or social background.

N. Secure participants' medicals, parent/guardian permission and liability waivers, and send each participant a personal-equipment list.

Phase III: Operational

A. Familiarize all participants with camp rules and emergency procedures.

B. Emphasize safety and camp hygiene at all times.

C. Provide structure to camp activities, but not regimentation.

D. Schedule daily activities to provide a balance of physical exercise, counselling, quiet introspection, nature appreciation, cultural studies, food growing and gathering, and co-operative group activities.

E. Exercise flexibility in daily activities to take best advantage of weather conditions and unforeseen opportunities.

F. Set aside a regular period for staff meetings and conflict resolution.

G. Deal with participant conflicts at once — do not schedule for later resolution.

H. Never subject participants to activities and chores the staff do not take part in themselves.

I. Set staff schedules allowing for sufficient time off to prevent "burn-out."

J. Determine beforehand disciplinary action for dealing with camp infractions: i.e., stealing, fighting, alcohol/drug use, et cetera. Physical punishment should always be avoided.

K. Immediately terminate staff in the field for serious offenses: i.e., alcohol/drug use, assault, sexual offences, endangering the health or well-being of camp members. (Note: It is important that all staff undergo a police-records check prior to hiring, and that anyone convicted of a crime of a violent or sexual nature not be employed.)

L. Maintain regular communication between the camp and the program's community-based administrator.

M. Encourage evaluators and members of the sponsoring board to visit the camp.

N. Control the number of other visitors in and out of camp to better enhance the feeling of isolation and an extended-family social unit.
O. Pay special attention to participants on medication, with serious allergies, or with physical or mental handicaps.
P. Provide wholesome, nutritious meals, avoiding highly processed and refined foods as well as excessive sugar.
Q. Emphasize respect for the land and all living things, and treat very seriously unnecessary killings, animal abuse, and tree and landscape defacement.
R. Emphasize respect for all members of camp regardless of age, race, creed, sex, culture, social status, or physical/mental disabilities.

Phase IV: Post-operational

A. Close camp. Remove all garbage and food to discourage scavengers — bears, rats, insects — from frequenting the site.
B. Clean, inventory, and properly store all equipment at the camp location or in town.
C. Submit evaluations and annual report to all funding sources.
D. Prepare funding applications for the following year.
E. Host a program reunion inviting all participants, their families, community leaders, and funding sources to a potluck dinner, slide show, or video presentation of the summer program and participant speeches.
F. Provide for community-based follow-up programs for participants in need of a support structure back in their home environment.

Building a Rediscovery of your own requires determination, clear objectives, and strength of character — qualities apparent in many Rediscovery staff.

CHAPTER 3
REDISCOVERY: KEEPING THE CIRCLE STRONG

Rediscovery is a community. A community is nothing more and nothing less than a circle of people. In that circle there are children, there are elders, there are teachers, and there are dreamers. Part of what keeps the circle strong is knowing what all the people in it need. For those people who have worked as board members for a Rediscovery program, the needs of the members of the circle are often glaringly apparent. What can be done to strengthen the circle and to meet those needs is often obvious but unattainable.

It is ironic and sad that the greatest challenge facing Rediscovery in Canada and the United States, two of the world's wealthiest nations, is a shortage of funding. Most Rediscovery programs struggle from year to year to operate summer camps on a largely volunteer basis. The few staff on salary are generally poorly paid and the essential, year-round administrative work is almost never funded. The pressing need for follow-up programs to the summer camps for youth at risk and the desire for year-round Rediscovery are, at present, financially unattainable goals.

Exacerbating the problem of funding is the fact that Rediscovery programs are set up to serve the needs of underprivileged youth in communities and regions often economically depressed. Fee structures for camps are kept minimal to guarantee that local youth, and those most in need, have access to Rediscovery services. The average $10 per day fee does not ever come close to matching the real costs of the camps (approximately $85 to $100 Canadian per day), so each local Rediscovery sponsoring body is annually faced with the dilemma of raising the difference.

Rediscovery sponsoring societies are constantly having to undertake funding drives through raffles, lotteries, art auctions, bake sales, benefit dinners and dances, telethons, and door to door greeting-card sales. While there is considerable community support for these endeavours, the communities must rely on these same strategies to fund everything from the local fire truck to additional hospital beds. Donations by local service clubs, church groups, and businesses, while greatly appreciated, are also necessarily limited.

Perhaps the cruelest irony facing Rediscovery is that the secret to its success is also a major contributor to its financial hardships. Rediscovery's very insistence on integration — integration of troubled kids with those well adjusted, school drop-outs with scholastic achievers, native with non-native youth, elders with children, and boys with girls —means that it falls between the funding cracks in a society where segregation is the norm. So old people go to nursing homes to be lonely, children go to day-care to be with only other children; the psychologically disturbed go to institutions for the mentally ill, and so on. Government departments dealing with native people have money for native programs. Drug-dependency programs have money exclusively for those with drug problems. But no one finds money for programs that defy the labels and cross all the boundary lines.

NEW DIRECTIONS

As Rediscovery enters its second decade, the determination is greater than ever to help each program find secure financial roots. By purchasing this book, you have already contributed to that process. A major portion of the royalty on each sale goes to Rediscovery International Foundation's support of all Rediscovery-affiliated camps. Further private donations (all tax deductible) can be earmarked for the Rediscovery Trust Fund. Rediscovery Trust is administered by the Vancouver Foundation — Canada's largest community fund. The Vancouver Foundation, which has been of tremendous assistance to all British Columbia–based Rediscovery programs, has agreed to match monies raised for Rediscovery Trust to help build the fund as quickly as possible. Private donations can also be made to each Rediscovery-affiliated camp directly by using the addresses in this book.

Many other foundations have supported Rediscovery in the past: Chris Spenser Foundation, James Hand Foundation, Outreach Foundation, Koerner Foundation, Soaring Eagle Foundation, Threshold Foundation, and Van Deusen Foundation. Their continued support, and that of many others, will be required to move Rediscovery forward into its second decade on a secure financial footing.

What is it we are trying to achieve? We need a commitment by government, communities, and individuals. Your personal contribution, in the form of a tax-deductible donation or volunteer service, will keep the Rediscovery circle strong and make a difference to a child in need today.

Rediscovery, the pathways followed are ancient and respected, the directions pursued are new and innovative. What we as a modern society have had to offer our children has been something less than ideal. By helping youth to re-establish a connection with the earth, other cultures, and their own inner selves, Rediscovery can only serve to brighten all our tomorrows.

Rediscovery International Foundation
P.O. Box 1207, Station E
Victoria, British Columbia
Canada V8W 2T6
Telephone: (604) 383-4510

EPILOGUE
By Evan Adams

My parents grew up during the great TB epidemics that swept through reserves around the time of the Second World War. My father's earliest memories are of his people's desperate attempts to survive. Most did not. It is easy for me to see then how he could assume that our people and our way of life would not survive, so much was lost at that time.

He raised me with the belief that our language and culture would not survive into the next generation. Though I grew up in almost untouched wilderness, ocean and forests all around me, I was taught that even this — the very land we live upon — would eventually disappear.

Native people no longer face the life-threatening epidemics of the thirties and forties; however, we can still feel as threatened as my father once did, as did his father before him and his father before him, back to the time of contact. The governments of North America still covet the land of the native peoples — that is today's threat.

I can now see the world through my father's eyes with perhaps as much despair as he once had. After all, the loss of our land is as serious a threat to our culture as the loss of our people once was. However, one thing is clear: North America's native peoples, like the immigrants who have settled here, are here to stay. We are not dying off or submerging into the dominant culture, despite social and even, as in my case, parental pressures. I did not see that my culture was dying and have found no need to abandon it. It is alive and well.

Rediscovery has a pre-eminent role in this. It gives a "hands on" experience with the land and the culture that evolved from it. Hand in hand, nature and native culture can be experienced by the participants as part of their rediscovery of themselves. Perhaps this is why I have so much hope that my father did not. Rediscovery is proof of our health and our future in today's world. Not only does it take into consideration the need for cultural and personal discovery and the subsequent pride taken therein, it also considers not only the presence but the contributions of non-native people. With its strict non-racist policies, Rediscovery ensures that all can celebrate youth and culture together, not segregated

Ancient past and new future come together on Rediscovery. "There is room for all to share and become part of the new hope."

271

from each other, as in the past.

We can all move forward through Rediscovery, leaving behind the image of the native person as a shabby, misinformed, and victimized urban-dweller. We can also leave behind my father's notion that we would not survive into the next generation. Perhaps we can never return to the life of our ancestors, but that does not mean that we cannot have pride and hope right now. The people of Rediscovery programs exhibit this through their work; their hope and pride resounding onward, perpetuating itself in many. My own father's ideas have changed recently: he cried alongside his elders at the sight of a new generation dancing their ceremonials — something not seen since before the epidemic.

I encourage all of you to participate in these programs whenever and wherever possible. Though Rediscovery is designed for the benefit of youth, native and non-native, there is room for all to share and be a part of the new hope of native people.

Evan Adams, March 1989.
Evan Adams is Coast Salish, a professional actor and playwright, as well as a founding director of the Rediscovery International Foundation. Evan conducts workshops nationwide as a role model for the National Native Alcohol and Drug Abuse program.

ACKNOWLEDGEMENTS

It would be inappropriate, and I think presumptuous, for me to try singling out all the people who are responsible for this book. Without Rediscovery there would not be such a book, and a full list of the people' involved in Rediscovery's evolution over the past decade would easily fill volumes two and three. And it is not enough to credit merely the living, for Rediscovery's roots go back to countless generations of native people from many nations who viewed the land not as something they inherited from their forefathers, but something they were borrowing from their grandchildren. If it is possible to acknowledge all these people in words, then I would feel it only appropriate that those words be in Haida — the language of the people who inspired the first Rediscovery. "How-a Haada Laas." Thank you good people.

As it is not possible to thank each person individually for their contributions to Rediscovery, it would be remiss on my part to not personally acknowledge all those who directly contributed to this production. There are some whose sensitivity and imagination helped to develop, or directly influence, many of the activities outlined in this book. Credit is due to Athena George, Shirley Paulson, Alfie Jeffries, Wanagun, the late Jerry Brown, Judy Kerr, Guujaaw, Michael James, Jeff Hardy, Terence Kokol, and those trailblazers in acclimatization learning: Joseph Cornell, Garth Gilchrist, and Steven Van Matre.

I wish to thank Paul George for encouraging me to take on this project; the Western Canada Wilderness Committee for acting as publishers and supporting Rediscovery through generous royalties; the Lynn Canyon Ecology Centre for providing resource material; Donna Wilson for patience in typing and preparing the manuscript; Guujaaw, Yaku, Evan Adams, Frank Brown, Lorraine Fox Davis, Dan Alcock, Cathy Wilson, Dulcie McCallum, Ross Ramsey, and Randy Stoltmann for serving as consultants in reviewing and improving this manuscript; Bill Reid and David Suzuki for their inspiring forewords, and Evan Adams for his fitting epilogue; all the contributors who wrote the reports on the various Rediscovery Camps; Debbie Duncan and Leon Ridley for their wonderful and sensitive illustrations; and a huge "How-a" to Athena George for her labour of love in editing, advising, and encouraging this book into reality, and above all for keeping it fun.

Thom Henley, March 1989.

QUICK ACTIVITY INDEX

Most of the 80 activities contained in this book are designed for people of ten years and older. Use these symbols to find the specific type of activity you want. Ideal group size and materials needed are also included in the index.

Indoors or Outdoors

Outdoors Only

Group Bonding

Touch/Contact

Silly Fun

Energy Burner

Self-Expression

Personal Growth

Nature Immersion

Nature Study

Cultural Immersion

Cultural Study

Drama

Campfire

ACTIVITY GUIDE

ACTIVITY	MATERIALS	

BONDING

Circle Greeting/Cinnamon Roll	None
Trust Fall/Lift Turn	None
Human Knot	None
Red Shoe, Blue Shoe	None
Shed The Snake Skin	None
Ha, Ha, Ha!!!	None
Missing Link	None
Group Picnic	None
Dox-En-Eye	Stick (approx. 1 metre)
I Love You Darling	None
Pass A Clap	None
Two Truths And A Lie	None
A What? A What? A What?	Two different natural objects

SHARING AND CARING

Talking Feather	Eagle feather, crystal, or carved wooden staff

277

ACTIVITY GUIDE

ACTIVITY	MATERIALS
Stoneribs — The Mythical Role Model	Possibly a text of a recorded legend
Secret Friend	Paper, pen, box
Big Brother/Big Sister	Paper, pen, box
Lovable and Capable	Paper, pen, tape, safety pins
Story Stick	Firewood sticks
Centre Circle	None

LOOKING INWARD

Readings	Selections of poems, haikus, prose
Spirit Spot	Paper, pens, paints, felt pens, envelopes
Viewing Party	Tea pot, loose tea, treats
Self-Esteem Backpack	Relaxing music if indoors
The Solo/Vision Quest	Sleeping bag, two matches, potato, cooking pot, water if necessary

EXPLORING ROOTS

A Day In The Life Of The Village	Role cards, basket, costumes, other cultural props
Early Contact	Kerchiefs, butter knives, cultural values cards
Reversing History	Costumes and props for role play

GROUP SIZE	ACTIVITY SYMBOLS	PAGE NO
Any		61
Any		66
Any		66
8 or more		67
No more than 20-25		67
8 or more		71

Any		71
Any		74
2-3		75
No more than 4-6		77
Any		81

5 or more per village		90
5 or more per group		94
5 or more		98

ACTIVITY GUIDE

ACTIVITY	MATERIALS
Role Reversal	Flip chart and felt pens, or blackboard and chalk
Frontier/Homeland	Puzzle cards, flip chart and pen

SHARING TRADITIONS

Four-Fire Ceremony	Blankets, face paints
Native Crafts	Tools and natural supplies
Gambling Bones	Marked sticks, fruit or treats for prizes
Ring-On-A-String	Long string, ring, treats for prizes
This Is You	Five or six randomly-selected objects
Goghits In The Woods	Face paint, survey ribbon, vegetables, treats for prizes
Ceremony Night	Drums, costumes, torches, puppet-kites, talking staff
Medicine Wheel	Natural objects found on location

SEEKING THE SPIRIT

Sunrise Ceremony	None
Sacred Directions Run	Staffs or rock shrines, coloured cloth or paint, feathers, shells
Morning Purification	Bundles of soft evergreens (fir, hemlock, yew)

GROUP SIZE	ACTIVITY SYMBOLS	PAGE NO
Any		101
10-12		103

4 groups of 3 or more		109
Any		111
4 or more		114
10 or more		116
Any		117
8 or more		118
Any		120
8 or more		123

Any		125
Any		126
Any		130

ACTIVITY GUIDE

ACTIVITY	MATERIALS
Circle Hug	None
Talking To The Trees	Stethoscope optional

EXPLORING

Camera Kids	Nature photos, index cards, coloured pencils and pens
Lost Planet	Survey ribbon, toothpick flags, magnifying lenses
The Conundrum Hunt	Index cards, bug boxes, zip-lock baggies
Greet A Tree	Blindfolds
Big Foot	Coat hanger bigfoot prints, note pads, pens, magnifying lenses
Octopus Garden	Plastic tubes (.5 meter) with plexiglass or magnifying lens sealed over one end
Night Safari	Burnt cork, pen lights, 1 safety flashlight, candle lanterns
Stargazers	Possibly blankets to lie on

SENSING

Eagle Eyes	Binoculars (10x25), index cards, felt pens, string
Bear Nose	Samples of various forest scents
Deer Ears	Two blindfolds, deer-antler head piece (optional)
Touch Crawl	None

GROUP SIZE	ACTIVITY SYMBOLS	PAGE NO
Any		130
Any		131

Any		136
6-10		139
6-10		140
6-10		143
6-10		146
6-10		149
5-10		150
5-10		152

4-6		154
5-10		156
5-10		158
5-10		159

ACTIVITY GUIDE

ACTIVITY	MATERIALS
Taste Trail	Plastic bags to collect tea samples

CONNECTING

Energy Pyramids	Energy flow posters, animal and plant index cards, 6-8 tennis balls
Wanted Dead Or Alive	Note pads, pens
Prey On Prey	Animal and plant index cards, safety pins
Tide Pool Community	Paper, felt pens
Wolf Pack Territory	Scent oils: garlic, lemon, peppermint
Big Bad Wolf	Habitat cards, ink pad, paper, pens
Three's A Crowd	Cookies: two flavours
Hungry, Hungry Marten	None
Time Travellers	Hand-made passports, 16 laminated time period cards, stamps or stickers, stamp pad, pens and coloured pencils
Beach-Life Bingo	Animal/plant bingo cards, chips, box with names
Crazy Fate	Animal playing cards
Mystery Guess	Clues to animals, ballot box, paper and pens
Eagles and Ravens	True and false questions, same colour kerchiefs

GROUP SIZE	ACTIVITY SYMBOLS	PAGE NO
5-20		162

12-20		163
5-10		167
5-10		169
5-10		169
10 or more		173
10 or more		174
4-6		176
10 or more		179
4-6 to a group		181
Any		186
4-6		188
Any		190
10 or more		193

ACTIVITY GUIDE

ACTIVITY	MATERIALS	

COMMUNICATING

Wolf Howl/Bear Growl	Blindfolds, animal name cards
Echo Location	Blindfolds
Talk Of The Town	Role cards, personality cards, life situation cards, flip chart or blackboard

SURVIVING

Fire Building Contest	Matches, cup, tea bag, and pot of water
Expeditions	Quality equipment, safety gear, maps or charts, food and personal supplies
Emergency Survival	Matches, sleeping bags
Rabbit Roast	Domestic rabbits or wild game, rocks for tool-making, snare wire, matches

TUNING IN

Forest Blankets	None
Be A Tree	Background music if indoors
Nature's Orchestra	Music scores, pens, coloured felts or pencils
Shared Vision	Paper and pens

Group Size	Activity Symbols	Page No
8 or more		194
10 or more		196
10 or more		198

Group Size	Activity Symbols	Page No
6-10		202
4-6 to a group		204
4-6		209
6-10		212

Group Size	Activity Symbols	Page No
Any		213
Any		215
Any		216
Any		217

ABOUT THE AUTHOR

Thom Henley was one of the original organizers of the Rediscovery program on Haida Gwaii, for which he served as a program director for seven years. He also lobbied for thirteen years to preserve the South Moresby archipelago, at the southern end of Haida Gwaii. He co-authored *Islands at the Edge*, which won the Bookseller's Choice Award in British Columbia and became a national best seller. South Moresby was declared a National Park Reserve in 1986.

Thom Henley has travelled to over sixty countries, living and learning from indigenous people. He has been the recipient of five national and international conservation awards and is a director of the Canadian Nature Federation and the Sierra Club. In 1987, the University of New York awarded him with the prestigious Sol Feinstone Award for his work with Rediscovery and his role in the preservation of South Moresby. It was the first time the honour had ever been bestowed on a recipient outside the United States.

Thom Henley is currently involved in global strategies for protecting endangered tropical and temperate forests as well as their indigenous populations. He serves Rediscovery International as executive director.